FLORAL CROCHET

Edited by

Mary Carolyn Waldrep

DOVER PUBLICATIONS, INC., *NEW YORK*

To my mother,
for sharing her love of needlework with me.

CROCHET ABBREVIATIONS

bal	balance	rnd	round
bl OR blk	block	rpt	repeat
ch	chain	sc	single crochet
dc	double crochet	s dc	short double crochet
dec	decrease	sk	skip
d tr	double treble	sl st	slip stitch
h dc	half double crochet	sp	space
inc	increase	st(s)	stitch(es)
incl	inclusive	tog	together
lp	loop	tr OR trc	treble crochet
p	picot	tr tr	triple treble (yarn over hook 4 times)
pc st	popcorn stitch		

* (asterisk) or † (dagger) . . . Repeat the instructions following the asterisk or dagger as many times as specified.

** or †† . . . Used for a second set of repeats within one set of instructions.

Repeat instructions in parentheses as many times as specified. For example: "**(Ch 5, sc in next sc) 5 times**" means to work all that is in parentheses 5 times.

Published in Canada by General Publishing Company, Ltd., 30 Lesmill Road, Don Mills, Toronto, Ontario.

Published in the United Kingdom by Constable and Company, Ltd., 10 Orange Street, London WC2H 7EG.

This Dover edition, first published in 1987, is a new selection of patterns from: *Crocheted Bedspreads, Direction Book 2000*, published by the Lily Mills Company, Shelby, N.C., in 1948; *Decorating with Crochet, Direction Book 1800*, published by the Lily Mills Company in 1948; *Flower Garden Doilies, Design Book No. 52*, published by the Lily Mills Company in 1950; *Roses in Crochet, Crochet Design Book No. 71*, published by the Lily Mills Company in 1953; *Spreads That Are Different in Motifs Easy to Make, Star Book No. 68*, published by the American Thread Company, New York, in 1949; *Gifts, Novelties & Toys, Design Book No. 23*, published by the Lily Mills Company in 1949; *Crochet Gifts and Bazaar Novelties in D.M.C. Cottons, Vol. 405*, published by the D.M.C. Corporation in 1953; *Doilies, Book No. 12*, published by Royal Society, Inc., in 1951; *Correct Table Settings, Book No. 260*, published by The Spool Cotton Company, New York, in 1949; *Bedspreads and Tablecloths, Star Book No. 109*, published by the American Thread Company, n.d.; *Doilies, Design Book No. 67*, published by the Lily Mills Company in 1952; *Lily's Album of Crocheted Designs, Book 1200*, published by the Lily Mills Company in 1944; *Edgings: Crocheted, Tatted, Design Book No. 58*, published by the Lily Mills Company, n.d.; *Fair, Bazaar and Gift Crocheting, Design Book No. 63*, published by the Lily Mills Company in 1952; *Crochet for Today, Tomorrow and Always, Direction Book 1700*, published by the Lily Mills Company in 1947; *Doilies, Design Book No. 83*, published by the Lily Mills Company in 1958; *Doilies, Star Doily Book No. 104*, published by the American Thread Company in 1953; *Crochet Your Gifts, Book No. 212*, published by The Spool Cotton Company in 1944; *Doily Book, No. 137*, published by the American Thread Company, n.d.; *'County Fair' Crochet, Design Book No. 51*, published by the Lily Mills Company in 1950.

Manufactured in the United States of America
Dover Publications, Inc., 31 East 2nd Street, Mineola, N.Y. 11501

Library of Congress Cataloging-in-Publication Data

Floral crochet / edited by Mary Carolyn Waldrep.
    p.   cm.
Selected patterns from various publications of American thread companies published in the 1940s and 1950s.
    ISBN 0-486-25532-8 (pbk.)
    1. Crocheting—Patterns. 2. Decoration and ornament—Plant forms. I. Waldrep, Mary Carolyn.
TT820.F66   1987
746.43′4041—dc19

87-20295
CIP

Introduction

During the first half of the twentieth century and well into the second, America's thread companies produced thousands of instructional leaflets to promote their products. These 10¢–25¢ leaflets contained designs for tablecloths, bedspreads, edgings, placemats, centerpieces and many other types of crocheted lace.

By the beginning of the 1960s, this flood of instructional material had slowed to a trickle and the earlier leaflets soon disappeared. Today, because of renewed interest in crocheted lace, these old leaflets, and the patterns they contain, have become collector's items.

Floral motifs had always made up a respectable proportion of the designs in the leaflets, and in the 1940s and 1950s, the vogue for floral crochet reached its zenith. A whole garden of designs appeared, from simple, stylized depictions of flowers to elaborate three-dimensional blossoms. This book is a compilation of some of the best floral patterns from that period. Modern technology allows us to show them to you as they originally appeared. Many of the threads listed in the instructions are still available, but, if not, similar threads can easily be found. Be sure to buy enough thread of the same dye lot to complete your project, since dye lots can vary considerably in color.

For best results, you should have the same number of stitches and rows as indicated in the instructions. Before beginning a project, make a small sample of the stitch, working with the suggested hook size and desired thread. If your work is too tight, use a larger hook; if it is too loose, use a smaller hook.

To give your project a professional look, you should wash and block it. For large projects that are made of many units sewn together, you may find it easier to block the individual pieces before joining them. Use a neutral soap and cool water. Squeeze the suds through the crochet, but do not rub; rinse thoroughly. If desired, starch the crochet lightly. Using rustproof pins, pin the piece right side down on a well-padded surface. When the crochet is almost dry, press it through a damp cloth with a moderately hot iron. Do not allow the iron to rest on the stitches.

The terminology and hooks listed in this book are those used in the United States. The following charts give the U.S. names of crochet stitches and their equivalents in other countries and the approximate equivalents to U.S. crochet hook sizes. Crocheters should become thoroughly familiar with the differences in both crochet terms and hook sizes before starting any project.

The stitches used in the projects in this book are explained on page 47. A metric conversion chart is located on page 48.

STITCH CONVERSION CHART

U.S. Name	Equivalent
Chain	Chain
Slip	Single crochet
Single crochet	Double crochet
Half-double or short-double crochet	Half-treble crochet
Double crochet	Treble crochet
Treble crochet	Double-treble crochet
Double-treble crochet	Treble-treble crochet
Treble-treble or long-treble crochet	Quadruple-treble crochet
Afghan stitch	Tricot crochet

STEEL CROCHET HOOK CONVERSION CHART

U.S. Size	00	0	1	2	3	4	5	6	7	8	9	10	11	12	13	14
British & Canadian Size	000	00	0	1	–	1½	2	2½	–	3	–	4	–	5	–	6
Metric Size (mm)	3.00	2.75	2.50	2.25	2.10	2.00	1.90	1.80	1.65	1.50	1.40	1.25	1.10	1.00	0.75	0.60

Friendship Garden Bedspread

MATERIALS—Lily Homestead Crochet and Knitting Cotton Art. 131 in skeins or Art. 205 in balls:—SINGLE SIZE—28-sks. Ecru or 34-sks. White; or 23-balls Ecru or 28-balls White or Cream. DOUBLE SIZE—30-sks. Ecru or 37-sks. White; or 25-balls Ecru or 30-balls White or Cream. GAUGE—Each Block measures about 6¼″ square. For single size spread about 75″ x 106″, make 12 x 17 Blocks; for double size spread about 81″ x 106″, make 13 x 17 Blocks. Crochet hook size 10.

BLOCK—FLOWER—Ch 9, sl st in 1st st. Ch 1, 16 sc in ring, sl st in back lp of 1st sc. Ch 3, 4 dc in same st, remove hook, insert it back in top of 3-ch, catch lp and pull thru for a popcorn st, (ch 7, a 5-dc-pc st in back lp of next 2d sc) 7 times, ch 7, sl st in 1st pc st. * (1 sc, 1 hdc, 5 dc, 1 hdc and 1 sc) all in next lp, (1 sc, 1 hdc and 3 dc) in half of next lp, ch 9, sl st in last dc for a p, (3 dc, 1 hdc and 1 sc) in bal. of same lp. Repeat from * 3 times. Cut 6″ long, thread to a needle and fasten off on back. 2d FLOWER—Repeat as far as p on 2d

petal. Instead of 9-ch p, ch 4, sl st in one lp of st at end of a p on 1st Flower, ch 4, sl st back in last dc to complete p. (3 dc, 1 hdc and 1 sc) in bal. of petal, (1 sc, 1 hdc and 3 dc) in next lp, sl st in center dc on next petal on 1st Flower. Complete petal with 2 dc, 1 hdc and 1 sc. (1 sc, 1 hdc and 3 dc) in next lp, ch 4, sl st in next p on 1st Flower, ch 4, sl st back in last dc, (3 dc, 1 hdc and 1 sc) in bal. of lp. Complete Flower and fasten off. Make and join 2 more Flowers into a square. CORNER—* Join to 1st petal to right of joining of 2 Flowers, ch 4, tr tr (thread over 4 times) in joining of Flowers, (ch 5, sc in 2 lps of 5th ch st from hook for a p, ch 1, tr tr in same place with last tr tr) 6 times, dc in next petal, ch 6, dtr in corner p of same flower. Ch 5, turn, tr in next tr tr, ch 5, dtr in next tr tr, ch 6, tr tr in next tr tr, ch 6, dtr in next tr tr, ch 5, tr in next tr tr, ch 5, dtr in next tr tr, ch 7, sl st in corner p of Flower. Cut 3″ long. Turn and repeat from * on each side. After 4th corner, do not cut. EDGE—Ch 1, turn, * 7 sc in next sp, 1 sc in next st, (5 sc in next sp, 1 sc in next st) twice, 6 sc in next sp, 3 sc in one lp of corner st, 6

sc in next sp, 1 sc in next st, (5 sc in next st, 1 sc in next st) twice, 7 sc in next sp, 1 sc in flower p. Repeat from * around, working over ends left from Corners. Sl st in 1st 1-ch. ROW 2—Ch 6, dc in same st, ch 3, sk next 2 sc, sl st in next 2 sc, * ch 3, (dc, ch 3, dc) in next 3d sc, ch 3, sk 2 sc, sl st in next 2 sc. Repeat from * to 4th st from corner. Ch 3, (dc, ch 3, dc, ch 7, dc, ch 3, dc) all in next 3d (corner) sc, ch 3, sk 2 sc, sl st in next 2 sc. Repeat from * around. End with 3-ch, sl st in 3d st of 1st 6-ch. Fasten off.

2d BLOCK—Join Blocks in final row of Edge:—Instead of 1st 7-ch corner lp, make 3-ch, sl st in a corner lp on 1st Block, ch 3, dc back in same corner sc, ch 1, sl st in corresponding shell on 1st Block, ch 1, dc back in same sc, * ch 3, sk 2 sc, sl st in next 2 sc, ch 3, dc in next 3d sc, ch 1, sl st in next shell on 1st Block, ch 1, dc back in same sc. Repeat from * across to corner. Join corner the same as 1st one, then complete row.

Continue to make and join Blocks for desired size.

Block to measurements given.

Daffodil Vanity Set

MATERIALS—DAISY Mercerized Crochet Cotton, size 30—2 balls or skeins, White, Cream or Ecru. Crochet hook size 13.

LARGE DOILY—Ch 136, tr in 12th st, (ch 3, tr in next 4th st) 31 times to end of ch (32 sps). **ROW 2**—Ch 7, turn, tr in next tr, (ch 3, tr in next tr) 31 times across to 4th st of end ch. **ROW 3**—Ch 7, turn, tr in next tr, (ch 3, tr in next tr) 7 times, (ch 1, tr in 2d st of next sp, ch 1, tr in next tr) twice (4 half-sps made). (Ch 3, tr in next tr) 3 times, 3 tr in next sp, tr in tr (1 bl made), ch 3, tr in next tr, (3 tr in next sp, tr in tr) 3 times, (ch 3, tr in next tr) 3 times, (ch 1, tr in 2d st of 3-ch, ch 1, tr in tr) twice, (ch 3, tr in next tr) 9 times to 4th st of end 7-ch. **ROW 4**—Ch 7, turn, tr in next tr, 8 sps, 4 half-sps, 3 sps, 3 bls, 1 sp, 1 bl, 3 sps, 4 half-sps and 8 sps across. Continue, following Chart, thru Row 43. **END**—Ch 3, 3 dc in side-top of last tr, ** (3 dc in next sp, 1 dc in next st) 22 times, turn, (ch 2, tr) 6 times in 7th dc from hook, ch 2, sl st in next 6th dc. Ch 1, turn, (3 sc in next sp, sc in tr) 6 times, 3 sc in next sp, sl st in last dc, (3 dc in next sp, dc in next st) 3 times, turn, (ch 3, tr tr in next 2d sc on shell) 13 times, ch 3, sl st in next 12th dc. Ch 1, turn, (2 sc, ch 5, sl st in last sc for a p, and 2 sc) in each sp around, 1 sc in each tr tr. Sl st in last dc, * (3 dc in next sp, 1 dc in next st) 3 times, turn, (ch 6, tr tr between next 2 ps) 13 times, ch 6, sl st in next 12th dc. Ch 1, turn, (4 sc, a p and 4 sc) in each sp, 1 sc in each tr tr around, sl st in last dc. * Repeat from * to * but with 9-ch lps. Turn and work back with (5 sc, a p and 5 sc) in each sp, 1 sc in each tr tr. Repeat from * to * again but with 12-ch lps and with (7 sc, a p and 7 sc) in each sp. Repeat again with 15-ch lps, (8 sc, a p and 8 sc) in each sp. Repeat again with 18-ch lps, (10 sc, a p and 10 sc) in each sp, (3 dc in next sp, 1 dc in next st) twice, 4

dc in corner st. Turn and work a row of 21-ch lps and tr tr around, ending with a sl st in corner 3-ch at start of "End," Ch 1, turn, (12 sc, a p and 12 sc) in each sp, 1 sc in each tr tr around, sl st in last dc, 3 dc in same corner st, (3 dc in next sp, 1 dc in next st) across end, 7 dc in corner st. Repeat from **. End with 3 dc in 1st corner, sl st in 1st 3-ch. Cut 6 inches long, thread to a needle and fasten off on back.

SMALL DOILY—Ch 7, sl st in 1st st. Ch 8, tr in ring, (ch 2, tr in ring) 12 times, ch 2, sl st in 6th st of 1st 8-ch, ch 1, (3 sc in next sp, 1 sc in tr) repeated around, sl st in 1st 1-ch. **ROW 3**—Ch 10 for a tr tr, turn, (ch 3, tr tr in next 2d sc) 27 times, ch 3, sl st in 10th st of 1st ch. **ROW 4**—Ch 1, turn, (2 sc, a p and 2 sc) in each sp, 1 sc in each tr tr around, sl st in 1st 1-ch. **ROW 5**—Ch 10 for a tr tr, turn, (ch 6, tr tr between next 2 ps) 27 times, ch 6, sl st in 10th st of 1st ch. **ROW 6**—Repeat Row 4 but with (4 sc, a p and 4 sc) in each sp. Repeat Row 5 with 9-ch sps, Row 4 with (5 sc, a p and 5 sc) in each sp; Row 5 with 12-ch sps, Row 4 with (7 sc, a p and 7 sc) in each sp; Row 5 with 15-ch sps, Row 4 with (8 sc, a p and 8 sc) in each sp; Row 5 with 18-ch sps and Row 4 with (10 sc, a p and 10 sc) in each sp. Fasten off as before. Make 2 Doilies.

Stretch and pin doilies right-side-down in true shape. Steam and press dry thru a cloth.

6

Springtime Tablecloth

end left from last row. End with ch 2, sl st in 1st sc. Cut 6" long, thread to a needle and fasten off on back. **ROW 3**—Turn, sc in White in center leaf at one corner, ch 12, sc in next leaf, * ch 9, dc in center dtr in next shell, ch 9, sc in next leaf, ch 9, (dc, ch 11, dc) in next (corner) leaf, ch 9, sc in next leaf. Repeat from * around, ending with ch 9, dc in 1st corner leaf, ch 5, tr in 3d st of 1st ch-12. **ROW 4**—Ch 12, turn, dc in next ch-9 lp, * (ch 9, dc in next lp) repeated across to corner, ch 11, dc in same corner lp. Repeat from * around, ending with ch 9, dc in corner lp, ch 5, tr in 3d st of 1st ch-12. **ROW 5**—Ch 5, turn, 4 tr in last ch-5, (ch 9, dc in next lp) repeated around, with ch 9, (a 5 tr, ch 11, 5 tr shell) in corners. End with ch 9, 5 tr in 1st corner, ch 5, tr in top of 1st ch-5. Repeat Row 5 once. Fasten off. **Flower**—In Pink, ch 8, sl st in 1st ch. Ch 1, 12 sc in ring. In back lps only, sl st in 1st sc, (ch 2, 2 dc in same sc, 2 dc in next sc, ch 2, sl st in same sc, sl st in next sc) 6 times, ending with only 1 sc. Cut 8" long and use to sew flower on Block. Make one more flower each in Blue, Yellow and Lavender. Tack on Block in same color order, centering each on a dtr-shell between leaves in Green row. **No. 2**—**BLOCK**—Repeat to 2d corner in Row 6. Instead of corner ch-11, make * ch 5, sl st in one lp of center st of a corner lp on 1st Block, ch 5, 5 tr back in corner lp on 2d Block, * (ch 4, sl st in next lp on 1st Block, ch 4, dc back in next lp on 2d Block) repeated across to corner, ending with 5 tr in corner lp. Repeat from * to *, then complete as for 1st Block. Continue to make and join 16 rows of 21 Blocks, being careful to have the color placement of flowers the same in all Blocks.

EDGE—Join White to one corner, ch 5, a 2-tr Cluster in same lp, (ch 7, sl st in 5th ch from hook for a p, ch 3, a 3-tr Cluster in same corner lp) 3 times, * ch 1, (a 3-tr Cluster, ch 7, p, ch 3, a Cluster) all in next lp. Repeat from * around, making 4 Clusters in each corner (like 1st corner). Join and fasten off.

BLOCKING—Stretch and pin cloth right-side-down on curtain or quilting frames. Lay frames over an ironing board or padded table a section at a time. Steam and press dry each section thru a cloth until entire cloth is blocked.

MATERIALS—Lily MERCROCHET Cotton size 30:—Large Balls—18-balls White and 8-balls Bright Nile Green; Small Balls—7-balls each Dk. Yellow, Blue, Beauty Pink and Dk. Lavender. Crochet hook size 13. Size —70 x 92 inches.

BLOCK—(Size—4⅜" when blocked) —In White, ch 8, sl st in 1st ch. Ch 5, tr in ring, ch 3, holding back the last lp of each tr on hook, make 2 tr in ring, thread over and pull thru all lps on hook (a Cluster made), (ch 15, a 2-tr Cluster in ring, ch 3, a 2-tr Cluster in ring) 3 times, ch 15, sl st in 1st tr. Cut 3" long. **Leaves**—Turn, sk 1st 5 ch of one ch-15 lp, * 4 sc in Green across to center of lp, ch 9, a 3-dtr Cluster in 8th ch from hook, ch 4, sl st in Cluster for a p, ch 8, sl st at base of Cluster, (ch 8, a 3-dtr Cluster in starting st of ch-8 a ch-4 p, ch 8, sl st at base of Cluster) twice, sk these 3 leaves, sc in 1-ch sp before 1st leaf, 3 sc in same corner ch-15, ch 2, 7 dtr between next 2 Clusters, ch 2, sk 1st 5 ch of next ch-15 lp and repeat from * around, working over

Spring Rose Luncheon Set

MATERIALS REQUIRED:

DAISY Mercerized Crochet Cotton, Art. 65; Size 30:
2 skeins White;

or

Lily MERCROCHET Cotton, Art. 161; Size 20:
3 balls White;

(Sufficient for 1 Place Mat, 1 Bread and Butter Plate Mat and 1 Goblet Mat).

No. 13 Steel Crochet Hook.

GAUGE—6 sps - 1 inch; 6 rows - 1 inch.

PLACE MAT—(SIZE: 12 x 18 inches)—Ch 65 and starting at "A" on Chart, sk 1 st, sl st in next 4 ch (on which to work 1 added blk in next row), sk 3 ch, dc in next 27 ch (9 blks), ch 2, sk 2 ch, dc in next 10 ch (1 sp and 3 blks), ch 2, sk 2 ch, dc in next 16 ch (1 sp and 5 blks).

ROW 2—Ch 16, turn, sk 1 ch, sl st in next 4 ch, sk 3 ch, dc in next 3 ch, ch 2, sk 2 ch, dc in next 3 ch, dc in next 13 dc, ch 2, sk 2 dc, dc in next dc, 2 dc in next sp,

8

dc in next 10 dc, 2 dc in next sp, dc in next dc, ch 2, sk 2 dc, dc in next 7 dc, (ch 2, sk 2 dc, dc in next dc) 5 times, ch 2, sk 2 dc, dc over next 4 sl sts inserting hook at base of sl sts (1 added blk).

ROW 3—Ch 19, turn, sk 1 ch, sl st in next 10 ch (on which to work 3 added blks in next row), sk 3 ch, dc in next 5 ch, dc in next 4 dc, continue, following Chart, with 1 blk, 4 sps, 1 blk, 3 sps, (5 blks, 1 sp) twice, ch 2, sk 2 dc, dc over next 4 sl sts.

ROW 4—Ch 22, turn, sk 1 ch, sl st in next 10 ch, dc in next 8 ch, dc in next 4 dc, make 2 sps, 5 blks, 3 sps, 3 blks, 4 sps, 4 blks and 3 sps, ch 2, sk 2 dc, dc over next 10 sl sts.

ROW 5—Ch 16, turn, sk 1 ch, sl st in next 4 ch, sk 3 ch, dc in next 6 ch, ch 2, sk 2 dc, dc in next 13 dc, follow Chart across, ending with dc over 10 end sl sts.

ROW 6—Ch 13, turn, sk 1 ch, sl st in next 7 ch, sk 3 ch, dc in next 2 ch, follow Chart across ending with dc over 4 end sl sts.

ROW 7—Ch 13, turn, sk 1 ch, sl st in next 4 ch, sk 3 ch, dc in next 5 ch, complete row ending with dc over 7 end sl sts.

ROW 8—Repeat Row 6.

ROW 9—Repeat Row 7.

ROW 10—Ch 10, turn, sk 1 ch, sl st in next 4 ch, sk 3 ch, dc in next 2 ch, dc in next dc, complete row ending with dc over 4 end sl sts. Repeat Row 10 thru Row 14.

ROW 15—Ch 6, turn, sk 4 ch, dc in next 2 ch, dc in next dc. End as in last rows.

ROW 16—Ch 7, turn, sk 1 ch sl st in next 4 ch, sk 1st dc, dc in next 18 dc, complete row ending with 3 blks (10 dc) even.

ROW 17—Repeat Row 10. Follow Chart thru Row 33.

ROW 34—Ch 3, turn, sk 1st dc, dc in next 6 dc, complete row, ending even. Work **even** thru Row 81.

ROW 82—Ch 1, turn, sk 1st dc, sl st in next 3 dc, ch 3, 2 dc in next sp, dc in next dc, complete row. Follow

Chart for bal. of doily. Where sps are dropped at beginning of a row, ch 1, turn, sk 1st dc, sl st across until starting place of next row is reached. End with Row 114, fasten off.

BREAD AND BUTTER PLATE MAT—(SIZE: 7½ inches) —**ROW 1**—Ch 44 and starting at "A" on Chart, sk 1 ch, sl st in' next 10 ch, sk 3 ch, dc in next 30 ch.

ROW 2—Ch 22, turn, sk 1 ch, sl st in next 10 ch, sk next 3 ch, dc in next 8 ch, dc in next 7 dc, 4 sps, 2 blks, 3 sps and 2 blks

ROW 3—Ch 19, turn, sk 1 ch, sl st in next 7 ch, sk 3 ch, dc in next 8 ch, dc in next 7 dc, 1 blk, 3 sps, 6 blks, 1 sp and 6 blks.

ROW 4—Ch 13, turn, sk 1 ch, sl st in next 4 ch, sk 3 ch, dc in next 5 ch, dc in next 7 dc, complete row ending with 2 added blks over 7 sl sts.

ROW 5—Ch 10, turn, sk 1 ch, sl st in next 4 ch, sk 3 ch, dc in next 2 ch, dc in next 7 dc, complete row ending with 1 added blk made over 4 sl sts. Complete doily in same way, — thru Row 46, fasten off.

GOBLET MAT—(SIZE - 5 inches):
ROW 1—Ch 41, sk 1 ch and starting at "A" on Chart, sl st in next 7 ch, sk 3 ch, dc in next 15 ch, ch 2, sk 2 ch, dc in next 7 ch, ch 2, sk 2 ch, dc in 4 end ch.

ROW 2—Ch 16, turn, sk 1 ch, sl st in next 7 ch, sk 3 ch, dc in next 5 ch, dc in next dc, (make 1 sp, 3 blks) 3 times.

ROW 3—Ch 13, turn, sk 1 ch, sl st in next 4 ch, sk 3 ch, dc in next 3 ch, ch 2, sk 2 ch, dc in next 37 dc, 2 sps, 2 blks.

ROW 4—Ch 10, turn, sk 1 ch, sl st in next 4 ch, sk 3 ch, dc in next 2 ch, dc in next dc, make 3 sps, 5 blks, 5 sps, 4 blks, 1 sp and 1 blk. Complete doily in same way, — thru Row 30, fasten off.

Stretch and pin doilies right-side-down in true shape. Steam and press dry thru a cloth.

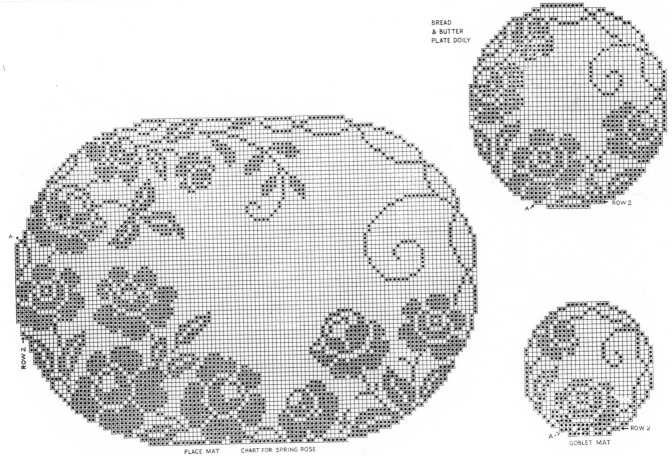

BREAD & BUTTER PLATE DOILY

← ROW 2

PLACE MAT   CHART FOR SPRING ROSE

ROW 2

ROW 2

GOBLET MAT

Rose Doily in Crocheted Tatting

MATERIALS REQUIRED:

DAISY Mercerized Crochet Cotton, Art. 65 (skeins)
1 skein Lt. Blue
and
1 skein Lt. Yellow.
Size 30:—

or

Lily MERCROCHET Cotton, Art. 161:—
2 balls Baby Blue and 1 ball Yellow, Size 20:—
No. 13 Steel Crochet Hook.
Size — 16 inches.

RING (R)—To form a Ring in Crocheted Tatting, make a chain of specified length marking one st with a pin as directed.

(EXAMPLE—Ch 38 marking 26th st with a pin). To do this ch 27 (one more st than the one to be marked). Put a pin in 2d ch from hook (the 26th st of ch), — pressing it down to the head. Continue the chain, counting from 28 thru 38. Remove hook from lp, remove pin, insert hook in marked ch st (the pin enlarges the st so it can be seen easily), catch lp at end of ch and draw thru to form a Ring out to left of chain.

CENTER ROSE—Starting in center with Lt. Blue ch 11, join with sl st to form a circle. Ch 1, 3 sc in circle, ch 3, sl st in last sc for a p, (2 sc in circle, p) 6 times, sc in circle, join with sl st in 1st sc, ch 1, hdc in same st for final p (8 ps).

RND 2—Ch 1, turn, sc in p, (ch 3, sc in next p) 7 times, ch 3, sl st in 1st sc.

RND 3—Ch 1, turn, sc in same st with sl st, (3 sc in next sp, sc in next sc) 7 times, 3 sc in next sp, sl st in 1st sc.

RND 4—Ch 1, turn, sc in same st, (ch 5, sc in next sc between lps) 7 times, ch 5, sl st in 1st sc.

RND 5—Ch 1, turn, sc in same st, (6 sc in next sp, sc in next sc) repeated around, join to 1st sc. Repeat Rnds 4 and 5 with these increases:

RNDS 6-7—Make 7-ch lps. 8 sc in each lp.

RNDS 8-9—9-ch lps. 10 sc in each.

RNDS 10-11—11-ch lps. 12 sc in each.

RNDS 12-13—13-ch lps. 15 sc in each.

RNDS 14-15—15-ch lps. 18 sc in each.

RNDS 16-17—17-ch lps. 21 sc in each.

RNDS 18-19—19-ch lps. 23 sc in each.

RNDS 20-21—21-ch lps. 25 sc in each.

RNDS 22-23—23-ch lps. 28 sc in each.

RNDS 24-25—26-ch lps. 31 sc in each.

RNDS 26-27—29-ch lps. 34 sc in each.

RNDS 28-29—32-ch lps. 37 sc in each.

RNDS 30-31—35-ch lps. 40 sc in each.

RND 32—38-ch lps.

RND 33—Ch 1, turn, sc in same st, * in next lp make (7 sc, ch 4, sl st in last sc for a p) 5 times and 7 sc; sc in next sc; repeat from * around, join to 1st sc. Fasten off.

SMALL ROSE—**Center**—Ch 10, join with sl st to form circle. Ch 3, 23 dc in circle, join to ch-3. Fasten off.
Petal—Ch 13, form a Ring (see directions above) in 13th ch from hook, ch 1, in R make (4 sc, ch 3, sl st in last sc for a p) 3 times and 4 sc; sl st in base of R.

RND 2—Ch 1, turn, sc in 1st p, (ch 5, sc in next p) twice, ch 5, sl st in base of R.

RND 3—Ch 1, turn, sc in same st, (7 sc in next sp, sc in next sc, a ch-3 p) 3 times, 7 sc in next sp, join with sl st in 1st sc.

RND 4—Ch 1, turn, sc in same st, (ch 9, sc in next p) 3 times, ch 9, sl st in 1st sc.

RND 5—Ch 1, turn, sc in same st, (12 sc in next sp, sc in next sc, a ch-3 p) 3 times, 12 sc in next sp, sl st in 1st sc, sl st in 1 dc on Center. Fasten off. Make 5 more petals, joining one to every 4th dc around Center.

Stamens—With Lt. Yellow ch 6, join with sl st to form circle. Ch 1, sc in ring, * draw out lp on hook ¼ inch long, insert hook in single back strand of long lp, thread over and draw thru, thread over and draw thru 2 lps on hook (Knot St made). Make another Knot St, sc in circle. Repeat from * 9 times. Fasten off. Sew in center of Small Rose. Make 8 Small Roses.

BORDER—Work around Center Rose from left-to-right.
RND 1—With Lt. Blue ch 13, form a R in 13th ch from hook, ch 1, in half of R make 4 sc, a ch-4 p, 4 sc keeping lp on hook, insert hook in center p on one section of Center Rose, thread over and draw thru p and lp on hook (joining-sl st made). Always make joinings in this way,— without removing hook from lp. In bal. of R make 4 sc, p, 4 sc; sl st in base of R. Mark this R with a safety pin. * Ch 38 marking 26th st with a pin, R in marked st, ch 1, (4 sc, p, 4 sc) in half of R, sk 1 p to right on Center Rose, join to next p, (4 sc, p, 4 sc) in bal. of R, sl st in base of R. Repeat from * around, joining a R to 1st, 3d and 5th ps on each section of Center Rose (24 Rs). Ch 25, join to 1st R.

RND 2—Work from right-to-left. Ch 1, in each lp around make (8 sc, p) 3 times and 8 sc. Join and fasten off.

RND 3—Repeat Rnd 1 of Border, joining 1st R to center p on lp to left of marked R, then join a R to center p on each lp around.

RND 4—Work from right-to-left. Ch 1, * (8 sc, p, 8 sc) in half of next lp, join to center p on 1 petal of a Small Rose, (8 sc, p, 8 sc) in bal. of lp, (8 sc, p, 8 sc) in half of next lp, join to next petal on same Small Rose, (8 sc, p, 8 sc) in bal. of lp, (8 sc, p, 8 sc) in half of next lp, ch 18, R in 18th ch from hook, ch 1, in R make 5 sc, p, (3 sc, p) 4 times and 5 sc; sl st in base of R; (8 sc, p, 8 sc) in bal. of lp; repeat from * around, join and fasten off.

FILL-IN MOTIF—Attach to 2d p to left of R between any 2 Roses, ch 23 marking 6th ch, R in marked st, ch 1, 6 sc in R, join to next p to right, 6 sc in R, join to 1st p on next R, (6 sc, p, 6 sc) in bal. of R, sl st in base of R, * ch 32 marking 15th ch, R in marked st, ch 1, 6 sc in R, join to last p on last R, 6 sc in R, join to next p on next R, 6 sc in R, ** p, 6 sc in R, sl st in base of R. Repeat from * twice and from * to ** again, join to next p on last Rnd, 6 sc in bal. of R, sl st in base of R, ch 5, join to next p on last Rnd.

RND 2—Ch 1, 6 sc in 1st ch-5 sp, (in next lp make 9 sc, p, 9 sc) 4 times, 6 sc in next sp, sl st in p. Fasten off. Repeat between all Roses.

EDGE—Attach to 1st free petal on one Rose, * (ch 22, sc in next petal) 3 times, ch 10, sc in 2d p on Fill-in Motif, ch 18, sc in next p, ch 10, sc in 1st free petal on next Rose. Repeat from * around, join.

RND 2—* In each of next 3 lps make (8 sc, p) 3 times and 8 sc; (6 sc, p, 6 sc) in next sp, in next lp make (6 sc, p) 3 times and 6 sc; (6 sc, p, 6 sc) in next sp. Repeat from * around, join and fasten off.
Stretch and pin doily right-side-down in a true circle. Steam and press dry thru a cloth.

Pansy Spread

Materials Required: AMERICAN THREAD COMPANY "DE LUXE" CROCHET AND KNITTING COTTON, ARTICLE 346 OR "PURITAN" BEDSPREAD COTTON, ARTICLE 40

39—250 yd. Balls Cream.

7—175 yd. Balls each of Shaded Lavenders and Shaded Yellows.

3—175 yd. Balls Green.

Each Motif measures about 10 inches.

40 Motifs, 4 x 10 are required for Spread measuring 40 x 100 inches without ruffle.

Steel Crochet Hook No. 8.

LAVENDER PANSY: With Shaded Lavenders, ch 7, join to form a ring, ch 3, 2 d c in ring, * ch 7, 3 d c in ring, repeat from * 3 times, ch 7, join in 3rd st of ch.

2nd Row. Sl st to loop, ch 3, 7 d c in same loop, ch 4, sl st in top of d c just made for picot, work 7 more d c in same loop, s c in center d c of 3 d c group, * 8 d c in next loop, ch 4, sl st in top of d c just made for picot, work 7 more d c in same loop, s c in center d c of 3 d c group, repeat from * once (3 petals), ch 4, 12 d tr c (3 times around hook) with ch 1 between each d tr c in next loop, ch 1, 2 tr c with ch 1 between in same loop, ch 1, 2 d c with ch 1 between in same loop, s c in center d c of next 3 d c group, 2 d c with ch 1 between in next loop, ch 1, 2 tr c with ch 1 between in same loop, ch 1, 12 d tr c with ch 1 between each d tr c in same loop, ch 4, join to base of 1st petal, break thread.

YELLOW PANSY: With Shaded Yellows, work 1st row same as 1st row of Lavender Pansy.

2nd Row. Sl st to loop, ch 3, 7 d c in same loop, ch 4, sl st in top of d c just made for picot, work 7 more d c in same loop, s c in center of 3 d c group, 8 d c in next loop, ch 4, sl st in top of d c just made for picot, work 7 more d c in same loop, s c in center of 3 d c group, 8 d c in next loop, ch 2, sl st in picot of 1st petal of Lavender Pansy, ch 2, sl st in top of d c just made, work 7 more d c in same loop, complete pansy in same manner as Lavender Pansy. Work 3 more Lavender and 3 more Yellow Pansies in same manner, joining same as 1st 2 pansies, alternating Colors, joining last Yellow Pansy to 1st Lavender Pansy.

Attach Cream in base of ch 4 of the 1st large petal of pansy, ch 3, skip 1 st, s c in next st of the ch 4, ch 3, s c over same ch 4 loop, * ch 3, s c in next ch 1 loop, repeat from * 14 times, * ch 3, s c in next ch 1 loop of next petal, repeat from * 14 times, ch 3, s c over ch 4 loop, ch 3, s c in 2nd st of ch, ch 3, sl st in base of ch 4, break thread.

Attach Cream in same manner to 1st large petal of next Pansy, ch 3, skip 1 st, s c in next st of the ch 4, ch 3, s c over same ch 4 loop, * ch 3, s c in next ch 1 loop, repeat from * once, ch 2, sl st in corresponding ch 3 loop of 2nd petal of previous pansy, ch 2, s c in next ch 1 loop, complete pansy same as 1st pansy and continue working all pansies in same manner, joining last pansy to first pansy.

CENTER JOINING MOTIF: With Cream, ch 5, join to form a ring, ch 1 and work 8 s c in ring, join.

2nd Row. Ch 8, sl st in 4th st from hook for picot, tr c in same space with ch 8, * ch 4, sl st in 4th st from hook for picot, tr c in next s c, ch 4, sl st in 4th st from hook for picot, tr c in same s c, repeat from * 6 times, ch 4, sl st in 4th st from hook for picot, join in 4th st of ch 8.

3rd Row. Ch 7, d c in next tr c, * ch 4, d c in next tr c, repeat from * 13 times, ch 4, join in 3rd st of ch 7, break thread.

4th Row. Attach Green, ch 1, ** 2 s c in mesh, ch 4, sl st in 4th st from hook for picot, 2 s c in same mesh, ch 7, sl st in 4th st from hook for picot, ch 3, join to picot of center petal of pansy, ch 7, sl st in 4th st from hook for picot, sl st in flat side of opposite picot, ch 3, sl st in top of last s c made, 2 s c, picot, 2 s c in next mesh, * ch 7, sl st in 4th st from hook for picot, repeat from * once, ch 3, join in joining between pansies, * ch 7, sl st in 4th st from hook for picot, join to opposite picot, repeat from * once, ch 3, sl st in top of last s c made, repeat from ** all around, join, break thread.

Join Cream in 2nd free loop to left of joining of Lavender Pansy, ch 7, skip 1 loop, d c in next loop, * ch 4, skip 1 loop, d c in next loop, repeat from * once, ch 4, skip 9 loops, d c in next loop of next petal, * ch 4, skip 1 loop, d c in next loop, repeat from * twice, d c in 2nd free loop of next pansy, ch 4, skip 1 loop, d c in next loop, repeat from first * all around, ending row with sl st in 3rd st of ch 7 (7 loops in each pansy).

2nd Row. Sl st to 2nd mesh, ch 1, * work 6 s c over each of the next 7 loops, ch 5, turn work, skip 11 s c, sl st in next s c, ch 1, turn and work 7 s c over loop just made, sl st in top of last s c in previous loop, repeat from * 6 times, complete row to correspond, join.

3rd Row. Sl st to 4th s c, ch 1, ** work 1 s c in each of the next 25 s c, * ch 7, s c in center of next scallop, repeat from * twice, ch 3, tr c in center of next scallop, ch 7, tr c in same space, ch 3, s c in center of next scallop, * ch 7, s c in center of next scallop, repeat from * once, ch 7, skip 6 s c, repeat from ** twice, complete row to correspond, join.

4th Row. Sl st to 4th s c, ch 1, ** work 1 s c in each of the next 19 s c, * ch 7, s c over next loop, repeat from * twice, ch 3, skip ch 3 loop, cluster st in next loop, (cluster st: * thread over hook twice, insert in loop, pull through and work off 2 loops twice, repeat from * twice, work off 2 loops, then work off remaining 3 loops at one time) ch 3, cluster st in same space, ch 5, 2 cluster sts with ch 3 between in same space, ch 3, s c over next ch 7 loop, ch 7, s c over next ch 7 loop, ch 7, s c over next loop, ch 7, skip 3 s c, repeat from ** twice, complete row to correspond, join in 1st s c.

5th Row. Sl st to 4th s c, ch 1, ** work 1 s c in each of the next 13 s c, * ch 7, s c over next loop, repeat from * twice, * ch 3, cluster st in next loop, repeat from * once, ch 3, 2 cluster sts with ch 3 between in next loop, ch 5, 2 cluster sts with ch 3 between in same loop, * ch 3, cluster st in next loop, repeat from * once, ch 3, s c in next loop, * ch 7, s c in next loop, repeat from * once, ch 7, skip 3 s c, repeat from ** twice, complete row to correspond, join in 1st s c.

6th Row. Sl st to 4th s c, ch 1, ** work 1 s c in each of the next 7 s c, * ch 7, s c over next loop, repeat from * twice, * ch 3, cluster st in next loop, repeat from * 3 times, ch 3, 2 cluster sts with ch 3 between in next loop, ch 5, 2 cluster sts with ch 3 between in next st, * ch 3, cluster st in next st, repeat from * 3 times, ch 3, s c over next loop, * ch 7, s c over next loop, repeat from * once, ch 7, skip 3 s c, repeat from ** twice, complete row to correspond, join in 1st s c.

7th Row. Sl st to center s c, work 1 s c in same space, * ch 7, s c over next loop, repeat from * twice, * ch 3, cluster st in next loop, repeat from * 5 times, ch 3, 2 cluster sts with ch 3 between in next loop, ch 5, 2 cluster sts with ch 3 between in same loop, * ch 3, cluster st in next loop, repeat from * 5 times, ch 3, s c over next loop, * ch 7, s c

(Continued on page 17)

13

Pansy Doily

MATERIALS — Lily Sil-Tone Mercerized Crochet Cotton:—1-ball each Purple and Shaded Reds, 1½-balls Cream. (Or use DAISY Mercerized Crochet Cotton Size 20:—1 partial ball or skein in Cream, 1 partial ball each of lavendar and shaded roses.) 1-sk. Lily Six Strand Floss in Lt. Green. Crochet hook size 10 or 11. A 9″ circle of linen.

In Cream, ch 7, dc in starting st, (ch 13, dc in 7th ch from hook) 39 times, ch 6 and with row untwisted, sl st in starting st. Sl st to center of 1st ch-7 lp. ROW 2—* (ch 6, sl st in 5th ch from hook for a p) twice, ch 10 and holding back on hook the last lp of each tr, make 2 tr in 6th ch from hook, thread over and draw thru all lps on hook at once (Cluster made), (ch 6, a 2-tr Cluster in 6th ch from hook) twice, dtr between 2d and 3d Clusters from hook, ch 6, a 2-tr Cluster in 6th ch from hook, sl st in end of next (1st) Cluster, ch 2, sl st in next 3d ch st, (ch 6, sl st in 5th ch from hook for a p) twice, ch 2, sc in next ch-7 lp in Row 1. (Ch 6, sl st in 5th ch from hook for a p) 7 times, ch 1, sc between 3d and 4th ps from hook, ch 5, p, sc between next 2 ps, ch 5, p, dc between next 2 ps, ch 5, p, ch 6, p, ch 2, sc in next lp of Row 1. Repeat from * around. Cut and fasten off on back. ROW 3—Sc between 2 top Clusters of 1st lp, * ch 7, p, (ch 6, p) 4 times, ch 3, sc in tip of next lp, ch 7, p, (ch 6, p) 4 times, ch 3, sc between 2 top Clusters of next lp. Repeat from * around. Cut and fasten off on back. ROW 4—Sc in center p of one lp, * ch 7, p, (ch 6, p) 4 times, ch 3, sc in center p of next lp. Repeat from * around. Cut and fasten off on back. Repeat Row 4 twice.

HEADING ROW—Join to a 6-ch sp in Row 1, ch 3, 5 dc in same sp, (dc in next st, a 2-dc-Cluster in next sp, dc in next st, 6 dc in next sp) repeated around. Join and fasten off.

PANSY—In Purple, ch 7, sl st in 1st st, * (ch 5, 5 dc in 5th ch from hook, ch 3, sl st in same ch, sc in ring) twice, * ch 6, 9 dc in 5th ch from hook, ch 3, sl st in same ch, sc in ring. Repeat from * to *. Cut 3″ long. Sc in Shaded Red down into ring working over last sc.

Working over Purple end left from last row, * make 1 sc and 2 hdc in 1st ch-3 lp on next petal, (2 hdc in one lp of next dc) 5 times, 2 hdc and 1 sc in next ch-3 lp, sc down into ring between petals. * Repeat from * to * once. Go around big petal in same way, with 2 hdc in one lp of each of the 9 dc. Then repeat from * to * on each remaining petal. Cut 8″ long, thread to a needle and tack petals tog. on back, lapping each small petal over next small petal to right, and lapping big petal up over each side petal. Make a Green French Knot in center. Make 20 Pansies and tack one on each 4-Cluster group in Row 2.

Stretch slightly and hem inside edge down on a true circle of linen. Working on back, cut linen ¼″ outside stitching, turn edge back against crochet and hem down on back of dc-row.

Stretch and pin doily right-side-down in a true circle on a padded board. Steam and press dry thru a cloth.

Pansies Refreshment Set

One 8-inch Doily and 4 Glass Muffs

MATERIALS — D·M·C Pearl Cotton, Art. 116D, Size 5: 7 balls Snow White or any desired D·M·C Color (A) and D·M·C Pearl Cotton, Art. 116D, Size 8: 1 ball Ombré No. 90 (B), 1 ball Ombré No. 58 (C). Steel Crochet Hook, Size 8.

GAUGE: 4 dc rows=1 inch

* = STAR

DOILY—With A ch 4, join (with slip st) into ring. **Rnd 1 (right side)**—Ch 3, work 17 dc in ring, join (in top ch of ch-3). **Rnd 2**—Ch 3 (=1 dc), 1 dc in joined st, 2 dc in each dc around, join. **Rnd 3**—Ch 3, skip joined st, 1 dc in each dc around, join. **Rnd 4**—Ch 3, 1 dc in joined st, 1 dc in next dc, * 2 dc in next dc, 1 dc in next dc; rpt from STAR around, join (54 dc). **Rnd 5**—Ch 3, 1 dc in joined st, 1 dc in each of 2 dc, * 2 dc in next dc, 1 dc in each of 2 dc; rpt from STAR around, join. **Rnd 6**—Ch 3, working in back loop of sts, 1 dc in joined st, 1 dc in each of 3 dc, * 2 dc in next dc, 1 dc in each of 3 dc; rpt from STAR around (leaving front loops of rnd 5 free), join (90 dc). **Rnd 7**—Ch 1, 1 sc in joined st, ch 5, * skip next dc, 1 sc in next dc, ch 5; rpt from STAR around, join in first sc (45 Loops). **Rnd 8**—Slip st to center of next Loop, ch 1, 1 sc in Loop, [ch 5 and 1 sc] in each remaining Loop; end, ch 5, slip st in first sc. Rpt rnd 8 five times. **Rnds 14 and 15**—Work as for rnd 8 only ch 6 instead of ch 5. **Rnds 16, 17 and 18**—Work as for rnd 8 only ch 7 instead of ch-5. **Rnd 19**—Slip st in next Loop, ch 3, 4 dc in same Loop, 5 dc in each remaining Loop, join. **Rnd 20**—Ch 1, 1 sc in each dc around, join in first sc. LOOP RUFFLE—**Rnd 1**—Ch 1, 1 sc in joined sc, * ch 10, skip next sc, 1 sc in next sc; rpt from STAR around; end, ch 10, skip next sc, join in first sc. **Rnd 2**—Ch 1, * 1 sc in free sc between next ch-10 Loop, ch 10; rpt from STAR around, join, fasten off. LOOP RUFFLE

AROUND CENTER—From right side, with A 1 sc in each free loop of rnd 5, join in first sc then work as for Loop Ruffle. Block and steam lightly. PANSY—Work 3 Pansies each of B and C. Sew in place as shown. **GLASS MUFF**—Base—Work to end of rnd 5 of Doily. Body—**Rnd 1**—Ch 3, skip joined st, 1 dc in back loop of each dc around (leaving front loops of rnd 5 of Base free), join in top of ch-3. **Rnd 2**—Ch 1, 1 sc in joined st, ch 5, * skip next 3 dc, 1 sc in next dc, ch 5; rpt from STAR around, join (in first sc). **Rnd 3**—Slip st to center of next Loop, ch 1, 1 sc in Loop, ch 5, [1 sc and ch 5] in each remaining Loop, join (18 Loops). Rpt rnd 3 ten times. **Rnd 14**—Work as for rnd 3 only ch 3 instead of ch-5. **Rnd 15**—Ch 3, skip joined st, 3 dc in next sp, * 1 dc in next sc, 3 dc in next sp; rpt from STAR around, join in ch-3. **Rnd 16**—Ch 1, 1 sc in joined st, 1 sc in each dc around, join then work same Loop Ruffle as for Doily. LOOP RUFFLE AROUND BASE—Holding top of Glass Muff toward you, work as for Loop Ruffle Around Center of Doily. Steam lightly. PANSY—Work 2 Pansies each of B and C. Sew in place as shown. Block to shape. **PANSY**—With A ch 6, join (with slip st) into ring. **Rnd 1**—Ch 3, 2 dc in ring, ch 8, * 3 more dc in ring, ch 8; rpt from STAR 3 times, join in top of ch-3. **Rnd 2**—Ch 1, skip joined st, 1 sc in next dc, 8 dc in next Loop, *ch 4, slip st in 5th st from hook (Picot made)*, 7 more dc in same Loop, 1 sc in center dc of next 3-dc group, [1 hdc, 8 dc] in next Loop, work a Picot (mark this Picot with thread), [7 dc, 1 hdc] in same Loop, 1 sc in center dc of next group, [8 dc, a Picot, 7 dc] in next Loop, 1 sc in center dc of next group, ch 5, [1 long tr (yo 3 times) and ch 1] in next Loop 13 times, [1 tr and ch 1] in same Loop twice, [1 dc, ch 1, 1 hdc] in same Loop, 1 sc in center dc of next group, [1 hdc, ch 1, 1 dc, ch 1, 1 tr, ch 1, 1 tr, ch 1] in next Loop, [1 long tr and ch 1] in same Loop 13 times, ch 4, join (in first sc), fasten off.

15

Pansy Wheel

ROYAL SOCIETY SIX CORD CORDICHET, Large Ball,

Size 30, 2 balls each of White, 1 ball each of (No. 3039) Ombre Lavender and (No. 3020) Nile Green.

Steel Crochet Hook No. 10.

A round piece of linen, 7 inches in diameter.

Doily measures about 18 inches in diameter.

Make a narrow hem all around linen. **1st rnd:** With White make 273 sc closely around edge of linen. Join with sl st to first sc made. **2nd rnd:** Ch 4, tr in next 4 sc, * (ch 3, skip 2 sc, tr in next sc) twice; ch 3, skip 2 sc, tr in next 5 sc. Repeat from * around. Join. **3rd rnd:** Ch 4, holding back on hook the last loop of each tr make tr in next 4 tr, thread over and draw through all loops on hook (cluster made), * ch 7, skip 1 sp, 5 tr in next sp, ch 7, holding back on hook the last loop of each st make

tr in next 5 tr, thread over and complete cluster as before. Repeat from * around. Join. **4th rnd:** * Ch 10, make a 5-tr cluster over next 5 tr, ch 10, sc in tip of next cluster. Repeat from * around, ending with ch 5, d tr in tip of cluster. **5th rnd:** * Ch 12, sc in next loop. Repeat from * around. Join and break off.

PANSY . . . Starting at center with Ombre Lavender, ch 6. Join with sl st to form ring. **1st rnd:** Ch 4, tr in ring,

* ch 5, holding back on hook the last loop of each tr make 2 tr in ring, thread over and draw through all loops on hook (cluster made). Repeat from * 3 more times; ch 5, sl st in first tr. **2nd rnd:** In next loop make sc, 2 dc, 2 tr, 2 dc and sc; in next loop make sc, 2 dc, tr, sl st in any ch-12 loop on Doily, in same loop on Pansy make tr, 2 dc and sc; in next loop make sc, 2 dc, 2 tr, 2 dc and sc; (in next loop make sc, dc, 2 tr, 5 d tr, 2 tr, dc and sc) twice. Join and break off. Make 20 more Pansies same as this, joining each Pansy to Doily as before, skipping one ch-12 loop between Pansies.

LEAVES . . . Skip 3 sts on first large petal on Pansy, attach Green to next st, sc in same st, * (ch 2, sc in next st) 7 times; sl st in next 2 sts on this petal and first 2 sts on next petal, sc in next st, (ch 1, sc in next st) 7 times; ch 10, sc in center st of next small petal, ch 2, sl st in 3rd ch preceding joining, ch 5, sc in next free loop on Doily, ch 5, sl st in same place as last sl st, ch 2, sc in /

(Continued on page 17)

16

Pansy Wheel

(Continued from page 16)

center of next free petal on next Pansy, ch 2, sl st in same place as last sl st, ch 5, sl st in 3rd ch of ch-10, ch 2, skip 3 sts on first large petal of Pansy, sc in next st. Repeat from * around. Join and break off.

Work in rnds over Pansies as follows: Skip two ch-1 loops on first petal of any Pansy. Attach White to next loop. **1st rnd:** * Ch 8, skip 2 loops, sc in next loop, ch 8, skip one loop on this petal and one loop on next petal, sc in next loop, ch 8, skip 2 loops, sc in next loop, ch 10, skip 2 loops on this petal and 2 loops on next petal, sc in next petal. Repeat from * around. Join **2nd rnd:** Sl st to center of loop, sc in same loop, * (ch 10, sc in next loop) twice; ch 5, 7 tr in next loop, ch 5, sc in next loop. Repeat from * around. Join. **3rd rnd:** Sl st to center of loop, sc in same loop, * ch 10, sc in next loop, ch 10, tr in next 7 tr, ch 10, skip ch-5 loop, sc in next loop. Repeat from * around, ending with ch 5, d tr in first sc made. **4th rnd:** * (Ch 10, sc in next loop) twice; ch 3, 2 tr in next tr, tr in next 2 tr, in next tr make tr, ch 3 and tr; tr in next 2 tr, 2 tr in next tr, ch 3, sc in next loop. Repeat from * around, ending with dc in d tr. **5th rnd:** Ch 9 (to count as tr and ch 5), sc in next loop, * ch 10, sc in next loop, ch 5, 2 tr in next tr, tr in next 4 tr, ch 3, tr in next sp, ch 3, tr in next 4 tr, 2 tr in next tr, ch 5, sc in next loop.

Repeat from * around. Join last tr to 4th st of ch-9. **6th rnd:** Ch 10, sc in next ch-10 loop, * ch 6, tr in next 6 tr, (ch 3, tr in next sp) twice; ch 3, tr in next 6 tr, ch 6, sc in next ch-10 loop. Repeat from * around. Join to 4th st of starting chain. **7th rnd:** Sl st in next 4 ch, sc in same loop, ch 9, sc in next loop, * tr in next 6 tr, (6 tr in next sp) 3 times; tr in next 6 tr, sc in next loop, ch 9, sc in next loop. Repeat from * around. Join. **8th rnd:** Sl st in next 4 ch, sc in same loop, ch 2, * (make a 6-tr cluster over next 6 tr, ch 9) 4 times; cluster over next 6 tr, ch 2, sc in next loop, ch 2. Repeat from * around. Join. **9th rnd:** Sl st to center of next ch-9 loop, sc in same loop, * ch 12, sc in next ch-9 loop. Repeat from * around. Join and break off. Starch lightly and press.

Pansy Spread

(Continued from page 13)

over next loop, repeat from * once, ch 7, skip 3 s c, s c in next s c, repeat from first * and complete row to correspond, join in s c.

8th Row. Sl st to center of loop, s c in same loop, * ch 7, sl st in 4th st from hook for picot, ch 3 (picot loop), s c in next loop, repeat from * twice, * picot loop, skip next ch 3 loop, s c in next loop, repeat from * 3 times, ch 11, s c in same loop, * picot loop, skip next ch 3 loop, s c in next loop, repeat from * 3 times, * picot loop, s c in next loop, repeat from * 3 times, repeat from 1st * twice, complete row to correspond, break thread.

Work a second motif joining it to 1st motif in the last row as follows: sl st to center of loop, s c in same loop, * ch 7, sl st in 4th st from hook for picot, ch 3 (picot loop), s c in next loop, repeat from * twice, * picot loop, skip next ch 3 loop, s c in next loop, repeat from * 3 times, ch 5, sl st in center st of corner loop of 1st motif, ch 5, s c in same space of 2nd motif, * ch 5, sl st in corresponding picot of 1st motif, ch 2, complete picot, ch 3, skip next ch 3 loop, s c in next loop of 2nd motif, repeat from * 3 times, ch 5, sl st in corresponding picot of 1st motif, ch 2, complete picot, ch 3, s c in next loop of 2nd motif, repeat from * 6 times, * ch 5, sl st in corresponding picot of 1st motif, ch 2, complete picot, ch 3, skip next ch 3 loop, s c in next loop of 2nd motif, repeat from * 3 times, ch 5, sl st in center st of corner loop of 1st motif, ch 5, s c in same loop of 2nd motif, complete motif same as 1st motif. Join the 3rd motif to 2nd motif and 4th motif to 1st and 3rd motifs in same manner. Work 36 more motifs joining in same manner.

With right side of work toward you, attach Cream in joining before corner, * ch 7, sl st in next picot, repeat from * 14 times, ch 7, sl st in 6th st of corner loop, ** ch 7, sl st in next picot. * ch 7, sl st in next picot, repeat from * 13 times, ch 7, sl st in joining st of next motifs, repeat from ** all around working all corners same as 1st corner, ending row to correspond.

RUFFLE BAND: With Cream, ch 11, d c in 8th st from hook, ch 2, skip 2 sts of ch, d c in next st, * ch 5, turn, d c in d c, ch 2, d c in 3rd st of ch, repeat from * until band measures 41 inches for end ruffle. Working across sides of meshes, work * 2 s c in one mesh, 3 s c in next mesh, repeat from * on both long sides of band, do not break thread.

1st Row of Ruffle. Ch 9, skip 1 s c, tr c in next s c, * ch 5, skip 1 s c, tr c in next s c, repeat from * across row having a multiple of 7 meshes, ch 12, turn.

2nd Row. S c in 1st mesh, * ch 8, s c in next mesh, repeat from * across row, ch 12, turn and work 15 more rows of ch 8 loops, ch 12, turn.

18th Row. Work 3 loops, ch 4, 3 tr c cluster st in next loop, ch 5, 3 tr c cluster st in same loop, ch 4, s c in next loop, * work 5-ch 8 loops, ch 4, 3 tr c cluster st in next loop, ch 5, 3 tr c cluster st in same loop, ch 4, s c in next loop, repeat from * across row ending row with 2-ch 8 loops, ch 12, turn.

19th Row. Work 2 loops, ch 4 and work 4 cluster sts with ch 5 between each cluster st in loop between next 2 cluster sts, ch 4, s c in next ch 8 loop, * work 4-ch 8 loops, ch 4, 4 cluster sts with ch 5 between each cluster st in loop between next 2 cluster sts, ch 4, s c in next ch 8 loop, repeat from * across row ending with 2-ch 8 loops, ch 12, turn.

20th Row. Work 2 loops, ch 4, skip 1 loop, 2 cluster sts with ch 5 between cluster sts in each of the next 3 loops, ch 4, s c in next ch 8 loop, * work 3-ch 8 loops, ch 4, skip 1 loop, 2 cluster sts with ch 5 between cluster sts in each of the next 3 loops, ch 4, s c in next ch 8 loop, repeat from * across row ending with 1 loop, ch 12, turn.

21st Row. Work 1 loop, ch 4, skip 1 loop, 2 cluster sts with ch 5 between cluster sts in each of the next 5 loops, ch 4, s c in next ch 8 loop, * work 2-ch 8 loops, ch 4, skip 1 loop, 2 cluster sts with ch 5 between cluster sts in each of the next 5 loops, ch 4, s c in next ch 8 loop, repeat from * across row ending with 1 loop, ch 12, turn.

22nd Row. Work 1 loop, * ch 4, skip 1 loop, 1 cluster st with ch 5 between cluster sts in each of the next 4 loops, ch 5, 2 cluster sts with ch 5 between in next loop, ch 5, 1 cluster st with ch 5 between cluster sts in each of the next 4 loops, ch 4, s c in next ch 8 loop, ch 4, s c in next loop, repeat from * across row ending row with 4, s c in last loop.

23rd Row. * Ch 7, sl st in 4th st from hook for picot, ch 3, (picot loop) s c in next loop, repeat from * 10 times, picot loop, skip next loop, s c in next loop and continue picot loops across row, break thread.

HEADING: Join Cream in 1st s c, ch 5, work 1 tr c with ch 1 between each tr c in each s c across row, ch 4, turn.

2nd Row. Sl st over ch 1 loop, * ch 4, sl st over next ch 1 loop, repeat from * across row, break thread.

Work 2 more ruffles in same manner having each band 101 inches in length.

Sew ruffle in position overcasting the center of band to outside edges of top section.

Irish Lace Luncheon Set

MATERIALS: J. & P. Coats Tatting-Crochet, Size 70, 4 balls of Beauty Pink . . . Steel Crochet Hook No. 14 . . . 1 yard of pink organdy.

PLACE MAT (Make 2)—First Motif . . . Starting at center, ch 8. Join with sl st to form ring. **1st rnd:** Ch 6, (dc in ring, ch 3) 5 times. Sl st in 3rd ch of ch-6. **2nd rnd:** In each sp make sc, half dc, 3 dc, half dc and sc (6 petals). **3rd rnd:** * Ch 5, sc between next 2 petals. Repeat from * around. **4th rnd:** In each loop around make sc, half dc, 5 dc, half dc and sc. **5th rnd:** * Ch 7, sc between next 2 petals. Repeat from * around. **6th rnd:** In each loop around make sc, half dc, 7 dc,

(Continued on page 20)

18

Garden Party Tea Cloth

90 x 110 Inches

MATERIALS: J. & P. Coats or Clark's O.N.T. Best Six Cord Mercerized Crochet, *Size 30:* **Small Ball:** J. & P. Coats—*40 balls of White or Ecru, or 49 balls of any color, or* Clark's O.N.T.—*61 balls of White or Ecru, or 74 balls of any color.* **Big Ball:** J. & P. Coats—*24 balls of White or Ecru, or 30 balls of any color . . . Steel Crochet Hook No. 10 . . . 4 yards of linen material 36 inches wide.*

GAUGE: Each motif measures 2¼ inches square.

CROCHETED SQUARE (Make 80)—First Motif . . . Starting at center, ch 10. Join with sl st to form ring. **1st rnd:** Ch 8, (tr in ring, ch 4) 7 times. Join to 4th ch of ch-8. **2nd rnd:** * Sl st in next sp, ch 4, 4 tr in same sp, ch 4, sl st in same sp. Repeat from * around. Join. **3rd rnd:** Sl st in next 4 ch, ch 4, tr in top of next ch, * ch 10, holding back on hook the last loop of each tr make tr in

(Continued on page 20)

19

Irish Lace Luncheon Set

(Continued from page 18)

half dc, and sc. **7th rnd:** * Ch 5, sc between next 2 petals of previous rnd. Repeat from * around, ending with sc between last and first petal. **8th rnd:** Ch 8, sc in 3rd ch from hook (picot made), * ch 3, dc in next loop, ch 3, picot, ch 3, dc in next sc, ch 3, picot. Repeat from * around, ending with ch 3, sl st in 3rd ch of ch-8. **9th rnd:** Sc in same place as sl st, * ch 2, picot, ch 5, picot, ch 2, sc in next dc. Repeat from * around, ending with sl st in first sc. Break off.

SECOND MOTIF . . . Work as for First Motif until 8th rnd is completed. **9th rnd:** Sc in same place as sl st, (ch 2, picot, ch 2, sl st in corresponding loop of First Motif, ch 2, picot, ch 2, sc in next dc on Second Motif) twice; and complete motif as for First Motif (no more joinings).

Make 7 more motifs, joining each motif to previous one as Second Motif was joined to First Motif, having 4 loops free on each side of joining.

HEADING . . . Attach thread to 4th free loop from last joining. **1st row:** Ch 5, d tr in same loop, * ch 9, sc in next loop, ch 5, sc in next loop, ch 9, holding back on hook the last loop of each d tr make 2 d tr in next loop, thread over and draw through all loops on hook (cluster made); make long tr (thread over hook 5 times) in joining between First and Second Motifs, make 2-d tr cluster in next loop. Repeat from * across, ending with ch 9, 2-d tr cluster in 4th loop of last motif. Ch 3, turn. **2nd row:** Dc in first loop, * ch 5, make a 2-dc cluster in next sp, (ch 5, make a 2-dc cluster in next sc) twice; ch 5, make a 2-dc cluster in next sp, ch 5, make a 2-dc cluster in next long tr. Repeat from * across. Break off. Work Heading on opposite side in same way.

Cut a piece of organdy 15 x 18 inches. Make a narrow rolled hem all around. Sew strip of motifs to one narrow edge.

EDGING . . . Attach thread to one corner on organdy, sc in same place, * ch 2, picot, ch 2, skip ¼ inch on organdy, sc in organdy over rolled edge. Repeat from *

around, working over crocheted strip to correspond. Join and break off.

NAPKIN (Make 2) . . . Make a motif as for First Motif, until 9th rnd is completed. Do not break off at end of 9th rnd. **10th rnd:** Sl st to center of next loop, ch 5. in same loop make d tr, ch 5 and 2-d tr cluster, * ch 9, sc in next loop, ch 5, sc in next loop, ch 9, in next loop make 2-d tr cluster, ch 5 and 2-d tr cluster. Repeat from * around. Join to top of first ch-5. **11th rnd:** Ch 3, dc in same place, * ch 3, 2-dc cluster in next sp, ch 3, 2-dc cluster in tip of next d tr cluster, ch 5, 2-dc cluster in next sp, (ch 5, 2-dc cluster in next sc) twice; ch 5, 2-dc cluster in next sp, ch 5, 2-dc cluster in tip of next d tr cluster. Repeat from * around. Join and break off.

Cut a piece of organdy 11½ inches square. Make a narrow rolled hem all around. Sew motif to one corner. Cut out organdy in back of motif. Turn ends under neatly. Sew in place. Make Edging same as for Place Mat.

Garden Party Tea Cloth

(Continued from page 19)

top of next 2 chains, thread over and draw through all loops on hook (joint tr made). Repeat from * around. Join last ch 10 with sl st to top of ch-4. **4th rnd:** * 12 sc in next sp, ch 1, 6 sc in next sp, ch 7, turn; d tr in next ch-1 sp, ch 7, skip 5 sc, sl st in next 2 sc, turn; 6 sc in next sp, ch 5, sc in 5th ch from hook (picot made), 4 sc in same sp, ch 7, 4 sc in next sp, picot, 6 sc in same sp, 6 sc in incompleted loop, ch 1. Repeat from * around. Join and break off.

SECOND MOTIF . . . Work as for First Motif until 3 rnds are completed. **4th rnd:** 12 sc in next loop, ch 1, 6 sc in next loop, ch 7, turn; d tr in ch-1 sp, ch 7, skip 5 sc, sl st in next 2 sc, turn; 6 sc in next loop, picot, 4 sc in same loop, ch 3, sl st in corresponding loop on First Motif, ch 3, 4 sc in next loop on Second Motif, ch 2, sl st in corresponding picot on First Motif, ch 2, sc in first ch of picot on Second Motif, 6 sc in same loop, 6 sc in incompleted loop, d tr in next ch-1 sp on First Mo-

tif, 12 sc in next loop on Second Motif, complete as for First Motif, joining next picot and next corner loop as before.

Make 2 more motifs, joining adjacent sides as Second Motif was joined to First Motif. To join corner loop of Fourth Motif to center, ch 3, sl st in corresponding loop of previous motif, ch 1, sl st in corresponding loop of First Motif, ch 3 and complete motif, making all other joinings as before. Block these motifs to measure 5 inches square.

LINEN SQUARE (Make 63) . . . Cut linen slightly larger than crocheted square to allow for hem. Make a narrow hem all around linen. Attach thread to one corner and sc closely around. Join and break off. Alternate motifs and linen squares diagonally as shown in illustration and tack in place.

Fill in between outer crocheted squares as follows: Work as for other motifs until 3 rnds are completed. **4th rnd:** 12 sc in next loop, ch 1, 6 sc in next loop, ch 7, turn; d tr in ch-1 sp, ch 7, skip 5 sc, sl st in next 2 sc, turn; 6 sc in next loop, ch 2, dc in corresponding picot preceding joining on

outer motif of a crocheted square, ch 2, sl st in first ch made, 4 sc in same loop on motif in work, ch 3, sl st in corresponding loop on next motif of crocheted square, ch 3, 4 sc in next loop on motif in work and complete motif, joining corresponding parts as before, being careful to join picot immediately following the 3rd corner loop with dc to corresponding picot of adjacent motif as first picot was joined. Fill in all spaces around outer edge the same way.

NAPKIN (Make 8) . . . Cut linen 15½ inches square. Make a narrow hem all around outer edges.

EDGING . . . Make a chain about 75 inches long. **1st row:** D tr in 11th ch from hook, * ch 7, skip 3 ch, sc in next ch, ch 7, skip 7 ch, sc in next ch, ch 7, skip 3 ch, d tr in next ch. Repeat from * across until piece measures slightly longer than outer edge of napkin, ending with ch 7, skip 7 ch, sc in next ch. Cut off remaining chain. Turn. **2nd row:** * 5 sc in next sp, in next sp make 5 sc, picot and 3 sc, ch 7, in next sp make 3 sc, picot and 5 sc. Repeat from * across. Break off.

Stained Glass Doily

ROYAL SOCIETY SIX CORD CORDICHET, Large Ball,
Size 30, 3 balls of White, 1 ball each of (No. 3011) Blue, (No. 3032) Dk. Yellow, (No. 3020) Nile Green, (No. 3037) Ombre Pink, and (No. 3039) Ombre Lavender.

Steel Crochet Hook No. 10.

Doily measures 14 inches square; each Motif measures 3½ inches square.

MOTIF . . . Starting at center with any color, ch 8. Join with sl st to form ring. **1st rnd:** 16 sc in ring. Join. **2nd rnd:** Sc in same place as sl st, * ch 4, skip 1 sc, sc in next sc. Repeat from * around. Join. **3rd rnd:** Sl st in next loop, ch 4, 6 tr in same loop, drop loop from hook, insert hook in top of ch-4, draw dropped loop through (popcorn st made), * ch 7, 7 tr in next loop, drop loop from hook, insert hook in first tr and complete a pc st. Repeat from * around. Join and break off. **4th rnd:** Attach White to any sp, sc in same sp, ch 24, * sc in 2nd ch from hook, ch 2, skip 1 ch, dc in next ch, (ch 2, skip 1 ch, tr in next ch) 10 times; sc in next sp on center (spoke made); ch 24, skip 5 tr on last spoke made, sl st in next tr. Repeat from * around. Join 6th tr on last spoke to sc on first spoke, complete last spoke, sl st in first sc. Break off. **5th rnd:** Skip 1 tr on any spoke, attach thread to next tr, sc in same place, * ch 18, skip 1 tr on next spoke, sc in next tr, ch 25, skip 1 tr on next spoke, sc in next tr. Repeat from * around. Join. **6th rnd:** Ch 4, * tr in next 18 ch, tr in next sc, tr in next 12 ch, 5 tr in next ch, tr in next 12 ch, tr in next sc. Repeat from * around. Join and break off. Make 15 more Motifs, varying colors for center.

JOINING . . . With right sides facing, place 2 motifs together and attach White to tr following center tr of any corner. Picking up back loop only and working through both thicknesses to join, make sc closely across side to tr preceding center tr of next corner. Break off.

Make 4 rows of 4 Motifs, joining adjacent sides as before.

EDGING . . . 1st rnd: With wrong side facing attach White to back loop of any tr, sc in each tr around, making 3 sc in center tr of each corner. Join and turn. **2nd rnd:** Ch 4, tr in back loop of each sc around, making 5 tr in center sc of each corner. Join and break off. Starch lightly and press.

Carnation Tablecloth

This tablecloth can be made with the following:
"GEM" CROCHET COTTON, Article 35, size 30
25 balls White, Med. Ecru or Dk. Cream or
"STAR" CROCHET COTTON, Article 20, size 30
34 balls White, Ecru or Dk. Cream.
Each motif measures about 3⅛ inches.
352 Motifs 16 x 22 are required for cloth measuring about 50 inches x 68 inches.
Steel crochet hook No. 12.

Ch 8, join to form a ring, ch 4, 2 tr c in ring keeping last loop of each tr c on hook, thread over and pull through all loops at one time, ch 5 and work 7 more cluster sts with ch 5 between each cluster st in ring (cluster st: thread over hook twice, insert in space, pull through and work off 2 loops twice, * thread over hook twice, insert in same space, pull through and work off 2 loops twice, repeat from * once, thread over and pull through all loops at one time), ch 5, join in top of 1st cluster st.

2nd Row: Ch 1, s c in same space, then work 5 s c over each loop and 1 s c in each cluster st, join.

3rd Row: * Ch 6, skip 2 s c, s c in next s c, repeat from * all around ending with ch 3, d c in same space as beginning, this brings thread in position for next row (16 loops).

4th Row: * Ch 6, s c in next loop, repeat from * all around.

5th Row: Sl st into loop, ch 4, 7 tr c in same loop, ch 3, s c in next loop, ch 3, * 8 tr c in next loop, ch 3, s c in next loop, ch 3, repeat from * all around, join in 4th st of ch.

6th Row: Ch 4, 1 d c in each of the next 7 tr c with ch 1 between each d c, * ch 2, tr c in next s c, ch 2, 1 d c in each of the next 8 tr c with ch 1 between each d c, ch 2, 1 tr c, ch 5, 1 tr c in next s c (corner), ch 2, 1 d c in each of the next 8 tr c with ch 1 between each d c, repeat from * twice, ch 2, tr c in next s c, ch 2, 1 d c in each of the next 8 tr c with ch 1 between each d c, ch 2, 1 tr c, ch 5, 1 tr c in next s c, ch 2, join in 3rd st of ch.

7th Row: Sl st to next d c, ch 4, 1 d c in each of the next 5 d c with ch 1 between each d c, * ch 4, s c in next tr c, ch 4, skip 1 d c, 1 d c in each of the next 6 d c with ch 1 between each d c, ch 4, skip 1 loop, 1 tr c, ch 5, 1 tr c in next loop (corner), ch 4, skip 1 d c, 1 d c in each of the next 6 d c with ch 1 between each d c, repeat from * twice, ch 4, s c in next tr c, ch 4, skip 1 d c, 1 d c in each of the next 6 d c with ch 1 between each d c, ch 4, skip 1 loop, 1 tr c, ch 5, 1 tr c in next loop, ch 4, join in 3rd st of ch.

8th Row: Sl st to next d c, ch 4, 1 d c in each of the next 3 d c with ch 1 between each d c, * ch 4, s c in next loop, ch 5, s c in next loop, ch 4, skip 1 d c, 1 d c in each of the next 4 d c with ch 1 between each d c, ch 4, skip 1 loop, 4 tr c with ch 3 between each tr c in next loop (corner), ch 4, skip 1 d c, 1 d c in each of the next 4 d c with ch 1 between each d c, repeat from * twice, ch 4, s c in next loop, ch 5, s c in next loop, ch 4, skip 1 d c, 1 d c in each of the next 4 d c with ch 1 between each d c, ch 4, skip 1 loop, 4 tr c with ch 3 between each tr c in next loop, ch 4, join in 3rd st of ch.

9th Row: Ch 3, 1 d c in each of the next 3 d c keeping last loop of each d c on hook, thread over and pull through all loops at one time, * ch 5, d c in next loop, ch 5, d c in next loop, ch 5, d c in next loop, ch 5, 1 d c in each of the next 4 d c keeping last loop of each d c on hook, thread over and pull through all loops at one time, ch 5, tr c in next tr c, ch 5, tr c in next tr c, ch 5, 2 cluster sts with ch 7 between in next loop (corner), ch 5, tr c in next tr c, ch 5, tr c in next tr c, ch 5, 1 d c in each of the next 4 d c keeping last loop of each d c on hook, thread over and pull through all loops at one time, repeat from * all around in same manner ending to correspond, join, cut thread.

Work a 2nd motif in same manner joining it to 1st motif in last row as follows: ch 3, 1 d c in each of the next 3 d c keeping last loop of each d c on hook, thread over and pull through all loops at one time, ch 5, d c in next loop, ch 5, d c in next loop, ch 5, d c in next loop, ch 5, 1 d c in each of the next 4 d c keeping last loop of each d c on hook, thread over and pull through all loops at one time, ch 5, tr c in next tr c, ch 5, tr c in next tr c, ch 5, cluster st in next loop, ch 3, join to corresponding corner loop of 1st motif, ch 3, cluster st in same space of 2nd motif, ch 5, tr c in next tr c, ch 2, skip 1 loop of 1st motif, s c in next loop, ch 2, tr c in next tr c of 2nd motif, ch 5, 1 d c in each of the next 4 d c keeping last loop of each d c on hook, thread over and pull through all loops at one time, ch 2, skip 1 loop of 1st motif, s c in next loop, ch 2, d c in next loop of 2nd motif, * ch 2, s c in next loop of 1st motif, ch 2, d c in next loop of 2nd motif, repeat from * once, ch 2, s c in next loop of 1st motif, ch 2, 1 d c in each of the next 4 d c of 2nd motif keeping last loop of each d c on hook, thread over and pull through all loops at one time, ch 2, tr c in next tr c of 2nd motif, ch 2, skip 1 loop of 1st motif, s c in next loop, ch 2, tr c in next tr c of 2nd motif, ch 5, cluster st in next loop, ch 3, join to corner loop of 1st motif, ch 3, cluster st in same space of 2nd motif, ch 5, tr c in next tr c and complete row same as 1st motif.

Join all motifs in same manner.

EDGE: Attach thread at corner, ch 4, cluster st in same space, * ch 6, sl st in 4th st from hook for picot, ch 2, cluster st in same space, repeat from * once, ** ch 4, s c in next loop, ch 4, * cluster st in next loop, ch 6, sl st in 4th st from hook for picot, ch 2, cluster st in same space, ch 4, s c in next loop, ch 4, repeat from * 3 times, cluster st in next loop, ch 2, ch 4 picot, ch 2, cluster st in same loop, ch 4, s c in joining of motifs, ch 4, skip remainder of corner loop of next motif, cluster st in next loop, ch 6, sl st in 4th st from hook for picot, ch 2, cluster st in same loop, repeat from ** all around working 3 cluster sts with ch 2, ch 4 picot, ch 2 between each cluster st at corners.

Pink Aster

ROYAL SOCIETY SIX CORD CORDICHET, Large Ball,
Size 30, 1 ball each of (No. 3020) Nile Green, (No. 3018) Beauty Pink and (No. 3011) Blue.

Steel Crochet Hook No. 10.

Doily measures 13½ inches in diameter.

Starting at center with Nile Green, ch 8. Join with sl st to form ring. **1st rnd:** 16 sc in ring. Join. **2nd and 3rd rnds:** Sc in each sc around. Join. **4th rnd:** 2 sc in each sc around. Join. **5th and 6th rnds:** Sc in each sc around. Join. **7th rnd:** 2 sc in each sc around. Join. **8th and 9th rnds:** Sc in each sc around. Join (64 sc). **10th rnd:** Sc in same place as sl st, * ch 5, skip 1 sc, sc in next sc. Repeat from * around. Join. **11th to 15th rnds incl:** Sl st to center of next loop, sc in

same loop, * ch 5, sc in next loop. Repeat from * around. Join. **16th, 17th and 18th rnds:** Sl st to center of next loop, sc in same loop, * ch 6, sc in next loop. Repeat from * around. Join. **19th, 20th and 21st rnds:** Same as 16th rnd making ch-7 loops (instead of ch-6). **22nd rnd:** Sl st to center of next loop, sc in same loop, * ch 11, sc in 5th ch from hook (picot made), ch 6, sc in next loop. Repeat from * around. Join. **23rd rnd:** Sl st in next 6 ch and in picot,

ch 4, 6 tr in same picot, * ch 3, holding back on hook the last loop of each tr make 3 tr in next picot, thread over and draw through all loops on hook (cluster made), ch 3, cluster in same picot, ch 3, 7 tr in next picot. Repeat from * around. Join. **24th rnd:** Ch 4, tr in next 6 tr, * ch 3, skip next sp, in next sp make cluster, ch 3 and cluster; ch 3, tr in next 7 tr. Repeat from * around. Join. **25th rnd:** Ch 4, make a

(Continued on page 27)

24

Daisy Ring

ROYAL SOCIETY SIX CORD CORDICHET, Large Ball,
*Size 30, 2 balls each of (No. 3020) Nile Green and White, 1 ball each of
(No. 3030) Yellow and (No. 3032) Dk. Yellow.*

Steel Crochet Hook No. 10.

Doily measures 14½ inches in diameter.

Starting at center with Nile Green, ch 15. Join with sl st to form ring. **1st rnd:** Ch 3, 31 dc in ring. Join to top of ch-3. **2nd rnd:** Ch 4, * dc in next dc, ch 1. Repeat from * around. Join to 3rd ch of ch-4. **3rd rnd:** Sl st in next sp, * ch 5, tr in next sp, ch 1, tr in next sp, ch 5, sl st in next 2 sps. Repeat from * around. **4th rnd:** Sl st in next 4 ch and in next sp, ch 5, * tr in next sp, ch 1, tr in next sp, ch 5, tr in next sp, ch 1. Repeat from * around. Join to 4th ch of ch-5. **5th rnd:** Sl st in next sp, sc in same sp, * ch 7, sc in next sp, 7 sc in next sp, sc in next sp. Repeat from * around. Join. **6th rnd:** Sl st in next 3 ch and in loop, ch 4, holding back on hook the last loop of each tr make 3 tr in same loop, thread over and draw through all loops on hook (cluster made) * ch 7, skip 3 sc, tr tr in next sc, ch 7, 4-tr cluster in next loop. Repeat from * around. Join to tip of first cluster. **7th rnd:** In each sp around make 5 sc, ch 3 and 5 sc. Join. **8th rnd:** Sl st in next 5 sc and in ch-3 loop, ch 4, 3 tr in same loop, * ch 7, 4 tr in next loop. Repeat from * around. Join. **9th rnd:** Ch 4, tr in next 3 tr, * ch 8, tr in next 4 tr. Repeat from * around. Join. **10th and 11th rnds:** Repeat 9th rnd, making ch 9 between tr groups. **12th rnd:** * Ch 4, tr in next 2 tr, ch 4, sl st in next tr, ch 5, make a 4-d tr cluster in same tr, ch 4, 4-d tr cluster in next tr, ch 5, sl st in same tr. Repeat from * around, ending with 4-d tr cluster in same place as first sl st, ch 5, sl st in same place. **13th rnd:** Sl st in next 4 ch, ch 4, tr in next 2 tr and in top of ch-4, * ch 7, tr in next sp, ch 7, tr in top of next ch-4, tr in next 2 tr, tr in top of next ch-4. Repeat from * around. Join. **14th rnd:** Ch 4, tr in next 3 tr, * ch 9, tr in next tr, ch 9, tr in next 4 tr. Repeat from * around. Join. **15th rnd:** Ch 4, tr in next 3 tr, * ch 5, sc in next sp, ch 9, sc in next sp, ch 5, tr in next 4 tr. Repeat from * around. Join. **16th rnd:** Ch 4, tr in next 3 tr, * ch 9, skip next sp, tr in next sp, ch 9,

(Continued on page 27)

Anemone

MATERIALS—Lily MERCROCHET COTTON:—Large Balls — 2-balls each Lavender and Shd. Pinks size 30, 2-balls White size 20; Small Balls — 2-balls Gray size 30. Lily Six Strand Floss:—4-sks Black. Sufficient for 4 place settings. Crochet hook size 13.

ANEMONE—In Lavender, ch 9, sl st in 1st st. Ch 1, 12 sc in ring. In back lps, sl st in 1st sc, * ch 3, 4 dc in same st. Ch 3, turn, dc in last dc, (2 dc in next dc) 3 times. Ch 3, turn, dc in last dc, tr in next 3 dc, ch 3, sl st in last tr for a p, tr in same dc, tr in next 2 dc, (dc, ch 3, sc) all in next dc, ch 5, sl st in same sc on center ring, sl st in back lps of next 2 sc. Repeat from * 5 times. Cut 6" long, thread to a needle and fasten off on back. Make a 2d row and tack on top of 1st row with petals between those of 1st row. **Center**—In Gray, * ch 6, (sl st, ch 5, sl st) all in 1st st of ch-6. Repeat from * 4 times. Sl st at base of 1st group. Cut 8" long and use to sew in center of flower. With Black Floss make a large French Knot in center,

winding 6 times around needle. **PLACE MAT**—(Size—13")—**Make 10** flowers each in Lavender and Shd. Pinks. Tack tog. by one petal on each side into a circle, alternating colors. **Center**—In size 20 White, ch 8, sl st in 1st ch. Ch 1, 10 sc in ring, sl st in 1st sc. Ch 15, tr in next sc, (ch 9, tr in next sc) 8 times, ch 9, sl st in 6th st of ch-15. **ROW 2**—(4 sc, ch 3, 4 sc) in each lp around. **ROW 3**—Sl st up to next point, (ch 13, sc in next point) repeated around. **ROW 4**—Sl st in next lp, ch 3, (5 dc, ch 5, 6 dc) in same lp, (6 dc, ch 5, 6 dc) in each lp around. Sl st in top of ch-3. **ROW 5**—Sl st in next 2 dc, ch 3, dc in each dc up point, * (3 dc, ch 5, 3 dc) all in next ch-5, dc in each dc down to 3d from angle, sk 4 dc in angle (2 on each side), dc in each remaining dc up point. Repeat from * around. Sl st in top of ch-3. **ROW 6**—Sl st in next dc, ch 3, dc in each dc up point, * (3 dc, ch 5, 3 dc) all in next ch-5, dc in each dc down to 2d from angle, sk 2 dc in angle (1 on each side), dc in each remaining dc up point. Repeat from * around. Sl st in top of ch-3. Repeat Rows 5,

6 and 5. **ROW 10**—Sl st in next 3 dc, ch 3, dc in next 9 dc, * (3 dc, ch 5, 3 dc) in ch-5, dc in 10 dc, ch 4, sk 6 dc in angle (3 on each side), dc in next 10 dc. Repeat from * around. End with ch 4, sl st in top of ch-3. **ROW 11**—Sl st in next 4 dc, ch 3, dc in next 8 dc, * (3 dc, ch 5, 3 dc) in ch-5, dc in 9 dc, ch 13, sk 4 dc on next point, dc in next 9 dc. Repeat from * around. End with ch 13, sl st in top of ch-3. **ROW 12**—Sl st in next 5 dc, ch 3, dc in next 6 dc, * (3 dc, ch 5, 3 dc) in ch-5, dc in next 7 dc, ch 13, sc in next lp, ch 13, sk 5 dc, dc in next 7 dc. Repeat from * around. Join to top of ch-3. **ROW 13**—Sl st in next 6 dc, ch 3, dc in next 4 dc, * (3 dc, ch 5, 3 dc) in ch-5, dc in next 4 dc, (ch 14, sc in next lp) twice, ch 14, sk 6 dc in next 4 dc. Repeat from * around. Join to top of ch-3. **ROW 14**—Sl st to tip of point, * (ch 15, sc in next lp) 3 times, ch 15, sc in next point. Repeat from * around, making ch-7 and dtr for final lp. **ROW 15**—(Ch 15, sc in next lp) repeated around, making ch-7 and dtr for final lp. **Joining Row**—Ch 8, sl st in 1st free

(Continued on page 27)

Anemone

(Continued from page 26)

back petal of a pink flower, * ch 8, sc back in next lp, ch 8, sl st in next free back petal of same flower, ch 8, sc back in next lp, ch 8, sl st in 1st free back petal of next flower. Repeat from * around. Fasten off. **Edge**—Join White to 1st free back petal on outside of a flower, (ch 21, sc in next back petal of same flower, ch 21, sc in 1st free back petal of next flower) repeated around. Fasten off. **ROW 2**—Sc in one lp, * ch 16, 5 dc in 5th ch from hook, remove hook, insert it back in ch preceding these dc, catch lp and pull thru (popcorn st made), ch 3, sl st at base of pc st, ch 11, sc in next lp. Repeat from * around. Fasten off.

BREAD AND BUTTER DOILY—(Size—9")—Make 5 flowers in each color. Join as for Place Mat. **Center**—Repeat Rows 1 thru 4. **ROW 5**—Sl st in next 3 dc, ch 3, dc in next 2 dc, * (3 dc, ch 5, 3 dc) in ch-5, dc in next 3 dc, ch 9, sk 6 dc in angle dc in next 3 dc. Repeat from * around. Make ch 4, tr in top of ch-3 for final lp. **Joining Row**—Ch 7, sl st in 1st free back petal on one flower, * ch 7, sc back in next point, ch 7, sl st in next free back petal on same flower, ch 7, sc back in next ch-9 lp, ch 7, sl st in next free back petal on next flower. Repeat from * around. Fasten off. **Edge**—Repeat 1st Row of Place Mat Edge except make ch-23 lps. **ROW 2**—Sc in one lp, * ch 17, make a pc st as in Place Mat, ch 3, sl st at base of pc st, ch 12, sc in next lp. Repeat from * around. Fasten off.

GLASS DOILY—Make 3 flowers in each color. Tack tog. alternately into a circle, leaving only one back petal free on each flower on inside of circle. **Center**—In White, ch 2, 6 sc in 1st ch, sl st in 1st sc. Ch 12, dc in next sc, (ch 9, dc in next sc) 4 times, ch 9, sl st in 3d st of ch-12. **ROW 2**—(5 sc, ch 3, 5 sc) in each lp. **Joining Row**—Sl st up to tip of 1st point, ch 6, sl st in free back petal on one flower, (ch 6, sc back in next point, ch 6, sl st in free back petal on next flower) repeated around. Fasten off. **Edge**—Join White to 1st free back petal on outside of one flower, * (ch 19, sc in next back petal of same flower) twice, ch 19, sc in 1st free back petal of next flower. Repeat from * around. Fasten off. Repeat Row 2 of Edge on Place Mat.

Stretch and pin doilies right-side-down in true circle on a padded board. Steam and press dry thru a cloth.

Pink Aster

(Continued from page 24)

cluster over next 6 tr, * ch 5, sc in tip of cluster, ch 8, skip next sp, in next sp make 3-tr cluster, ch 3 and 3-tr cluster; ch 8, cluster over next 7 tr. Repeat from * around. Join. **26th rnd**: Sl st in picot, ch 4, 6 tr in same picot, * ch 5, skip next sp, in next sp make cluster, ch 3 and cluster; ch 5, 7 tr in next picot. Repeat from * around. Join. **27th rnd**: Ch 4, tr in next 6 tr, * ch 5, skip next sp, in next sp make cluster, ch 3 and cluster; ch 5, tr in next 7 tr. Repeat from * around. Join. **28th rnd**: Ch 4, cluster over next 6 tr, * ch 5, sc in tip of cluster, ch 11, skip next sp, in next sp make cluster, ch 3 and cluster; ch 11, cluster over next 7 tr. Repeat from * around. Join. **29th rnd**: Sl st in next picot, ch 4, 6 tr in same picot, * ch 8, skip next sp, 3 tr in next sp, ch 8, 7 tr in next picot. Repeat from * around. Join. **30th rnd**: Ch 4, tr in next 6 tr, * ch 8, tr in next 3 tr, ch 8, tr in next 7 tr. Repeat from * around. Join. **31st rnd**: Ch 4, cluster over next 6 tr, ch 5, sc in tip of cluster, * ch 12, cluster over next 3 tr, ch 12, cluster over next 7 tr, ch 5, sc in tip of cluster. Repeat from * around. Join. **32nd rnd**: Sc in picot, * (ch 4, tr in same picot, ch 4, sc in same picot) 3 times; 14 sc in next sp, sc in next cluster. Repeat from * around. Join and break off.

FLOWER (Make 16) . . . Starting at center with Blue, ch 8. Join with sl st to form ring. **1st rnd**: 16 sc in ring. Join to first sc. **2nd rnd**: Sc in front loop of same sc, * ch 3, skip 1 sc, sc in front loop of next sc. Repeat from * around. Join. **3rd rnd**: In each loop around make sc, 3 half dc and sc. Join and break off. **4th rnd**: Attach Pink to back loop of first sc on first rnd, sc in same place and in each sc around. Join to first sc. **5th rnd**: Sc in front loop of same sc, * ch 4, 2 tr in same sc, ch 4, sc in front loop of next 2 sc. Repeat from * around. Join. **6th rnd**: Sc in back loop of each sc around. Join. **7th rnd**: Sc in each sc around. Join. **8th rnd**: * Ch 4, 4 tr in same sc as sl st, ch 4, sl st in same sc, 2 sc in next 2 sc, sl st in next sc. Repeat from * around. Join and break off. Sew flowers around doily. Starch lightly and press.

Daisy Ring

(Continued from page 25)

tr in next 4 tr. Repeat from * around. Join. **17th rnd**: Ch 4, tr in next 3 tr, * ch 10, tr in next tr, ch 10, tr in next 4 tr. Repeat from * around. Join. **18th rnd**: Ch 4, tr in next 3 tr, * ch 10, tr in next tr, ch 4, 3 tr in last tr made, ch 4, sl st in same tr, ch 10, tr in next 4 tr. Repeat from * around. Join and break off.

FIRST MOTIF . . . Starting at center with Dk. Yellow, ch 4. **1st rnd**: 13 dc in 4th ch from hook. Join. **2nd rnd**: Ch 3, dc in same place as sl st, 2 dc in each dc around. Join and break off. **3rd rnd**: Attach White to any dc on 2nd rnd, sc in same place, * ch 12, dc in 4th ch from hook and in each ch across, skip next dc on 2nd rnd, sc in next dc. Repeat from * around. Join and break off. **4th rnd**: Attach Yellow to first dc made on any petal, sc in same place, ch 2, sc in base of 3rd dc on next petal, ch 8, sl st in top of first ch-4 of any tr group on doily, ch 4, sl st in 4th ch of ch-8, ch 4, sc in first dc on same petal, ch 2, sc in base of 3rd dc on next petal, ch 8, sl st in center of next tr group, ch 4, sl st in 4th ch of ch-8, ch 4, sc in first dc on same petal, ch 2, sc in base of 3rd dc on next petal, ch 8, sl st in top of next ch-4 of next tr group, ch 4, sl st in 4th ch of ch-8, ch 4, * sc in first dc on same petal, ch 2, sc in base of 3rd dc on next petal, ch 7. Repeat from * around. Join and break off.

SECOND MOTIF . . . Work as for First Motif until 3 rnds are completed. **4th rnd**: Attach Yellow to first dc made on any petal, sc in same place, ch 2, sc in base of 3rd dc on next petal, ch 3, sl st in 2nd free loop following joining on First Motif, ch 3, sc in first dc on same petal on Second Motif, ch 2, sc in base of 3rd dc on next petal, ch 3, sl st in next loop on First Motif, ch 3, sc in first dc on same petal on Second Motif, ch 2, sc in base of 3rd dc on next petal, ch 8, sl st in top of first ch-4 on same tr group as First Motif was joined, ch 4, sl st in 4th ch of ch-8, ch 4, sc in first dc on same petal, ch 2, sc in base of 3rd dc on next petal, ch 8, sl st in center of next tr group, ch 4, sl st in 4th ch of ch-8, ch 4, sc in first dc on same petal, ch 2, sc in base of 3rd dc on next petal, ch 8, sl st in top of next ch-4 on next tr group, ch 4, sl st in 4th ch of ch-8, ch 4, sc in first dc on same petal, ch 2, sc in base of 3rd dc on next petal. Complete rnd as for First Motif.

Make 14 more motifs, joining corresponding loops as Second Motif was joined to First Motif and to Doily. Join corresponding loops on last motif to First Motif. Starch lightly and press.

Forget-Me-Not Swirl Doily Set

MATERIALS REQUIRED:

DAISY Mercerized Crochet Cotton, Art. 65:—

3 skeins White *and*

5 skeins Med. Blue size 30; *or*

DAISY Mercerized Crochet Cotton, Art. 97:—

4 balls White *and*

7 balls Med. Blue size 30; *or*

Lily MERCROCHET Cotton, Art. 161:—

4 balls White *and*

7 balls Med. Blue size 30; *and*

Lily Six Strand Floss:—

16 skeins Dp. Yellow (sufficient for 4 Place Mats, 4 Bread and Butter Plate Doilies and 4 Glass Doilies).

Steel crochet hook No. 13.

PLACE MAT—(Size:—In DAISY—16 inches; in MERCRO-CHET—14 inches)—

Starting in center with White, ch 9, join with sl st to form ring. *1st rnd*—Ch 1, 14 sc in ring, join with sc in 1st sc. *2d rnd*—Ch 5, dc in next sc, (ch 4, tr in next sc) twice, (ch 4, dtr in next sc) twice, (ch 4, tr tr in next sc) 6 times, (ch 4, a long tr in next sc) twice. To make a long tr, thread over 5 times, insert hook in next sc, thread over and draw thru sc, (thread over and draw thru 2 lps on hook) 6 times. Drop this thread, but do not cut. *2d Thread*—Join a 2d ball of thread to next sc, 3 sc and 3 hdc in next ch-5 sp, dc in next dc, (5 dc in next sp, dc in next st) 11 times. Drop this thread. *1st Thread*—Pick up 1st Thread, ch 4, a long tr in 1st sc on next ch-5 sp, (ch 4, a long tr in next st) twice, (ch 4, sk 1 dc, a long tr in next dc) 17 times. (Mark last long tr with a small safety pin to help in counting). (Ch 4, sk 2 dc, a long tr in next dc, ch 4, sk 1 dc, a long tr in next dc) 6 times. (Mark final long tr with pin). Drop this thread. *2d Thread*—* (4 dc in next sp, dc in next long tr) repeated around to 2d long tr from end of last row. Drop this thread. * *1st Thread*—(Ch 4, sk 2 dc, a long tr in next dc) 27 times. (Mark final long tr). (Ch 4, sk 3 dc, a long tr in next dc, ch 4, sk 2 dc, a long tr in next dc) 12 times. (Mark final long tr). Drop this thread. Repeat from * to *. *1st Thread*—**** (Ch 4, sk 3 dc, a long tr in next dc, ch 4, sk 2 dc, a long tr in next dc) 35 times. (Mark final long tr). Drop this thread. *2d Thread*—Repeat from * to *. *1st Thread*—*** (Ch 4, sk 3 dc, a long tr in next dc) 90 times around to 2d dc from end of last row. (Mark final long tr). Drop this thread. *2d Thread*—Repeat from * to *. *1st Thread*—(Ch 4, sk 3 dc, a long tr in next dc) 100 times. (Mark final long tr). Drop this thread. *2d Thread*—Repeat from * to *. *1st Thread*—** Ch 4, sk 4 dc, a long tr in next dc, (ch 4, sk 3 dc, a long tr in next dc) twice. ** Repeat from ** to ** around to 6th dc from end of last row. (Mark final long tr). Drop this thread. *2d Thread*—Repeat from * to *. *1st Thread*—Repeat from ** to ** around to 12th dc from end of last row. (Mark final long tr). Drop this thread. *2d Thread*—Repeat from * to *. *1st Thread*—Repeat from ** to ** around to 13th dc from end of last row. (Mark final

long tr). Drop this thread. *2d Thread*—Repeat from * to *. *1st Thread*—Repeat from ** to ** 6 times. (Mark final long tr). (Ch 4, sk 4 dc, a long tr in next dc, ch 4, sk 3 dc, a long tr in next dc) 46 times. Fasten off this thread. *2d Thread*—(4 dc in next sp, dc in next long tr) repeated around last row, 5 dc in end long tr, 12 dc over bar of same long tr, sk next 2 dc in row below, sl st in next dc. Fasten off.

FLOWER BRAID—With Blue, ch 8, join with sl st to form ring. (Ch 3, 2 dc in ring, ch 3, sc in ring) 4 times, ch 3, holding back the last lp of each dc on hook, make 3 dc in ring, thread over and draw thru all 4 lps on hook (Cluster made). *2d FLOWER*—Ch 9, hdc in 6th ch from hook, drawn down tightly, forming a ring, ch 3, 2 dc in ring, ch 3, sc in ring, ch 3, dc in ring, sl st in top st of 3 ch between flowers, turn work around in a counter-clockwise direction, keeping same side facing and keeping hook on side facing, so that uncompleted flower is to left and previous flower is to right. Ch 3, sc in ring, (ch 3, 2 dc in ring, ch 3, sc in ring) twice, ch 3, a 3-dc Cluster in balance of ring for 5th petal. Continue as for 2d Flower for required length. Sew 1st Flower on ring in center of doily, then sew Braid around and around on dc-row out to end of spiral and across end of last row. With Yellow Floss make a large French Knot in center of each Flower.

BREAD AND BUTTER PLATE DOILY—(Size:—In DAISY —7 inches; in MERCROCHET—6½ inches)—Repeat to ***. (Ch 4, sk 3 dc, a long tr in next dc) 23 times. Fasten off. Work dc-row around and end as for Place Mat. Repeat Braid.

GLASS DOILY—(Size:—In DAISY—5½ inches; in MERCROCHET—5 inches)—Repeat to ****. (Ch 4, sk 3 dc, a long tr in next dc, ch 4, sk 2 dc, a long tr in next dc) 7 times. Fasten off. Work dc-row around and end as for Place Mat. Repeat Braid.

Stretch and pin doilies right-side-down in true circle. Steam and press dry thru a cloth.

Tea Rose Card Table Cover

A table cover you will take pride in using — for either small luncheons, teas, or that snack after a bridge game.

MATERIALS—2-skeins DAISY Mercerized Crochet Cotton, size 30, in White or a color. 1-square yard colored or white linen. Crochet hook size 10.

SPRAY—Rose—Ch 7, sl st in 1st st. Ch 10, dtr in ring, (ch 3, dtr in ring) 10 times, ch 3, sl st in next 7th st. **ROW** 2—Ch 1, * (sc, ch 2, 3 dc, ch 2, sc) in next 3-ch, sc in dtr. Repeat from * around, sl st in 1st 1-ch. **ROW 3** —(Ch 5, sc between next 2 shells) around. **ROW 4**—Ch 2, sc in next loop, ch 3 for a dc, * ch 3, dtr in next loop, (ch 3, tr tr) 4 times in same loop, ch 3, dtr in same loop, ch 3, dc in next loop. Repeat from * around. Join final 3-ch to 1st 3-ch. **ROW 5** — Ch 3, (dc in next 3-ch, dc in dtr) worked off together into a Cluster, * (4 dc in next 3-ch, dc in tr tr, ch 4, sl st in last dc for a p) 4 times, 4 dc in next 3-ch, (dc in dtr, dc in 3-ch, dc in dc, dc in 3-ch, dc in dtr) made into a Cluster. Repeat from * around. End with a 2-dc-Cluster, sl st in 1st Cluster. Fasten off. **LEAF**—Ch(6, dc in 6th st from hoop) 9 times, ch 8, sl st in 8th st from hook, (sc under bar of next dc, ch 4, sl st at base of same dc) 9 times. **ROW** 2—Ch 5, (dc, ch 2, tr) in next loop, ch 2, (dtr, ch 2, dtr) in next, * ch 2, (tr tr, ch 2, tr tr) in next loop. Repeat from * 3 times. Ch 2, (dtr, ch 2, dtr) in next loop, ch 2, dtr in next, ch 2, tr in next, (ch 2, dc) 5 times in end loop, ch 2, (tr, ch 2, tr) in next loop up other side, ch 2, dtr in next, ch 2, (dtr, ch 2, dtr) in next, (ch 2, tr tr in next) 5 times, ch 2, (dtr, ch 2, tr) in next, ch 5, sl st in end st. **ROW 3**—Ch 3, 6 dc in next 5-ch, (dc in next st, 3 dc in next sp) twice, dc in dtr, dc in next sp, a 4-ch p, dc in same sp. Continue around with 2 dc in each sp, 1 dc in each st between, putting a p in every 7th dc. In tip end dc, make (3 dc, p, 2 dc). After 13th p, make 2 dc in next sp, dc in tr tr, 3 dc in next sp, dc in dtr, a p, 3 dc in next sp, dc in tr, 6 dc in end sp, (sl st, ch 3, dc) in 1st 3-ch. Fasten off. Tack stem between 2 petals on flower, and sew to flower ps on each side. Make a 2d leaf thru Row 2. Turn over and make Row 3, reversing order of ps. Tack to opposite side of flower. Make 16 sprays (3 for each side, 4 in center). Make 4 Sprays more for corners, but leave only 2 Flower petals between leaf joinings. Make a cardboard pattern slightly larger than Sprays. Mark around this on tissue paper. Stretch and pin each Spray right-side-down on a tissue pattern, and steam and press dry thru a cloth. Arrange Sprays around edge of linen and in a center circle, pinning in place. Tack together where they meet. Working on right side, whip outside edge of Sprays to linen. Turn work over, cut linen ¼″ from stitching, turn edge back next crochet and hem down on back of dc-row on edge of Sprays. Press linen smooth.

Flower Edgings

DOILY—ROSE EDGING
(Illustrated at right above)

MATERIALS—Lily Mercrochet Cotton size 20:—1-ball each in Yellow, Dk. Yellow and Hunter Green. (DAISY Mercerized Crochet Cotton size 20 in skeins of colors desired may be used if preferred). Crochet hook No. 12. Size —13½ inches. A 10" circle of Yellow Linen.

ROSE—With Dk. Yellow, ch 6, join with sl st to form ring. *ROW 1*—Ch 7, dc in ring, (ch 4, dc in ring) 3 times working over starting end. Ch 4, join with sl st in 3d ch of ch-7. *ROW 2*—Ch 1, sc in same ch, * ch 2, 5 dc in next ch-4 sp, ch 2, sc in next dc. Repeat from * 4 times. *ROW 3*—(Ch 5, sc in back lp of sc between next 2 petals) 5 times. *ROW 4*—* Ch 2, (dc, 5 tr, dc) in next ch-5 lp, ch 2, sc in next sc. Repeat from * 4 times. Fasten off. Make 20 Roses.

MOTIF—Sc in Green in center st of one petal, ch 13, dc between petals, ch 8, dc between next 2 petals, (ch 4, tr, ch 4, dc) in same place, ch 8, dc between next 2 petals, ch 8, tr in center st of next petal, ch 8, sk 1 tr, dc in next tr, ch 8, dc in 3d st on next petal, ch 8,

sk 1 tr, dc in next tr, ch 8, dc in 2d st on next petal, ch 8, join with sl st in 5th ch of ch-13. *ROW 2*—Ch 1, sc in same st, (8 sc in next lp, sc in dc) twice, 4 sc in next lp, (sc, ch 3, sc) in next tr, 4 sc in next lp, sc in dc, (8 sc in next lp, sc in next st) twice, ch 4, sl st in last sc for a p. (5 sc, a p, 4 sc) in each of next 5 lps, join to 1st sc, * ch 4, sl st in same sc. Fasten off. *2d MOTIF*—Repeat 1st Motif to * in Row 2. Sl st in 2d p made on 1st Motif. Fasten off. Make and join Motifs into a circle.

HEADING ROW—Sc in Yellow in ch-3 p at top point of one Motif, * ch 6, sk 5 sc, tr in next sc, ch 5, sk 5 sc, tr in next sc, ch 5, holding back the last lp of each tr on hook, sk 5 sc and make tr in next sc and a tr in 6th sc on next Motif, thread over and draw thru all lps on hook (Cluster made), ch 5, sk 5 sc, tr in next sc. Ch 5, turn, sk Cluster in angle, (tr in next 2 tr) made into a Cluster. Ch 6, turn, sk Cluster, (tr in next tr, sk 5 sc on Motif, tr in next sc) made into a Cluster, ch 6, sk 5 sc, sc in next ch-3 p. Repeat from * around. Join. *ROW 2*—Ch 3, * (2 dc, a 2-dc Cluster and 2 dc) in next lp, dc between lps. Repeat from * around.

Join to top of ch-3. Fasten off. *ROW 3* —Sc in Green in same st, (ch 5, sk 2 dc, sc in next dc) repeated around. *ROW 4*—Sl st to center of next lp, ch 3, hdc in next lp, (ch 2, hdc in next lp) repeated around. Join to ch-3. Fasten off. *ROW 5*—Sc in Lt. Yellow in one hdc, ch 3, * 2 dc in next sp, dc in next hdc, a 2-dc Cluster in next sp, dc in next hdc. Repeat from * around. Join to ch-3. Fasten off.

Stretch and pin lace right-side-down in a true circle. Steam and press dry thru a cloth. Baste over linen circle. Hem inner edge of lace down closely. Cut cloth ¼" outside stitching, turn edge back next to lace and hem down on back of dc-row.

FORGET-ME-NOT EDGING
(Illustrated at upper center)

MATERIALS—Lily Mercrochet Cotton size 30 in Shd. Blues and Bright Nile Green (DAISY Mercerized Crochet Cotton size 30 may be substituted if preferred); Lily Six Strand Floss in Dk. Yellow. Crochet hook No. 13. Size— 1½ inches.

(Continued on page 33)

Flower-Trimmed Pillowcases

Crocheted "Cutwork" Pillowcase

MATERIALS REQUIRED:
DAISY Mercerized Crochet Cotton size 30.
1-skein each No. 23S Shd. Roses and No. 21S Shd. Greens.
Steel crochet hook No. 13.
A pair of white pillow cases.
*BORDER—Flower—*With Shd. Greens, ch 8, join with sl st to form ring. *ROW 1—*Ch 1, 12 sc in ring, join with sl st in back lp of 1st sc. *ROW 2—** Ch 4, 5 dc in same sc, remove hook, insert it back in ch preceding these 5 dc, catch lp and draw thru (popcorn st made), ch 3, sl st in same sc with pc st, sl st in back lp of next 2 sc. Repeat from * around (6 pc sts). Join and fasten off. *ROW 3—*Join Shd. Roses between any 2 pc sts, ch 11, * dtr in back lp of next pc st, ch 8, dtr in same place, ch 6, tr in next sc between pc sts, ch 6 and repeat from * around (6 petals). Join final ch-6 to 5th st of ch-11. *ROW 4—*3 sc, 2 hdc and 3 dc in next ch-6 sp, * 3 dc in next sp, ch 5, sl st in last dc for a p, (3 dc, a p) twice in same sp, 3 dc in bal. of same sp, 3 dc, 2 hdc and 3 sc in next sp, 3 sc in 1st sp on next petal, sl st back in 3d st up previous petal, 2 hdc and 3 dc back in same sp on 2d petal. Repeat from * around, join and fasten off. Tack 1st and 6th petals tog. by 3d st up side of each.
*Leaf—*With Shd. Greens, ch 8, tr in 8th ch from hook, ch 7, sl st in same st. *ROW 2—*Sc in next ch-7 lp, ch 6, tr in same lp, (ch 6, dtr) twice in same lp, ch 6, tr tr in next tr, (ch 6, dtr) twice in next ch-7 lp, ch 6, tr in same lp, ch 6, sc in left end of same lp. *ROW 3—** Sc in next ch-6 sp, (ch 1, 3 dc, ch 1, sc) twice in same sp. * Repeat from * to * 3 times. Ch 1, 2 dc in 1 lp of next tr tr, ch 3, sl st in last dc for a p, dc in same tr tr, ch 1 and repeat from * to * 4 times. Ch 10 for a stem, sk 1 ch, sl st in next 9 ch, join to next sc on leaf. Fasten off.
Rip out hem of pillow case, press out creases. Tack stems of 3 leaves to 1 petal of a flower. Tack leaves tog. where they touch and to next petal on each side of flower. Pin these groups around pillow case with a flower between groups as in illustration. Baste motifs in place, then hem down inner edge of Border. Cut cloth ¼ inch from stitching, turn edge back against crochet and hem down on back of edge of motif. Steam and press dry on back thru a cloth.

Floral Appliqué Pillowcase

MATERIALS REQUIRED:
DAISY Mercerized Crochet Cotton size 30.
1-skein each No. 60 Lt. Green, No. 15S Shd. Pinks, No. 18S Shd. Lavenders and No. 19S Shd. Yellows.
Steel crochet hook No. 13.
A pair of white pillow cases.
Rip out hem of pillow case, press out creases.

EDGING—Braid—With Lt. Green, * (ch 6, dc in 6th ch from hook) 13 times to measure 3¼ inches, ch 18, remove hook, insert back in starting st of ch-18, catch lp and draw thru, forming a ring out to left side of work. Repeat from * 13 times (14 scallops). With row untwisted, join to starting end. *ROW 2*—Working back, make * sc in large lp. In same lp make (ch 1, 7 dc, ch 1, sc) 3 times, 3 sc in next dc-sp, (sc between dc, 3 sc in next dc-sp) repeated across to next large lp. Repeat from * around. *ROW 3*—* Ch 4 behind next large lp, sl st in 1st 2 sc on next sp, (ch 3, sk 1 sc, sc in next sc) repeated across to large lp. Repeat from * around. Fasten off.

Edge—Working on other side of Braid, join Green to 1st ch-5 lp on 1 section, ch 8, tr in next lp, * (ch 5, tr in next lp) 10 times, ch 3, tr in next (end) lp, tr in 1st lp on next section, ch 3, tr in next lp. Repeat from * around. Join final tr to 5th st of ch-8. *ROW 2*—Ch 5, sl st in same place for a p, 3 sc in next sp, * (3 sc, a p, 3 sc) in each ch-5 sp across section, 3 sc in end ch-3 sp, a p, 3 sc in next section. Repeat from * around, join and fasten off.
Mark each half of pillow case into 7 equal sections. With a large lp on each mark, baste Edging in even scallops around case. Hem inner edge down closely, cut cloth ¼ inch from stitching, turn this edge back against crochet and hem down on back of Braid.
FLOWER—With Shd. Pinks, ch 5, dc in 4th ch from hook, ch 3, sl st in same st, sc in next ch (center ch of flower), (ch 4, dc in 4th ch from hook, ch 3, sl st in same st, sc in same center st) 4 times (5 petals). *ROW 2*—(Ch 3 behind petal, sc in next sc between petals) 5 times. *ROW 3*—* Ch 4, 3 tr in next ch-3 lp, ch 4, sc in same lp, ch 4, 2 tr in same lp, 1 tr in next lp, ch 4, sc in same lp, ch 4, 3 tr in same lp, ch 4, sc in same lp. Repeat from * once. Ch 4, (3 tr, ch 4, sc) in next lp. Fasten off. With Green, make a large French Knot in center. Make 1 Flower each in Shd. Yellows and Shd. Lavenders.

STEM—With Green, ch 20, * sc in 2d ch from hook, hdc in next ch, dc in next ch, tr in next 3 ch, dc in next ch, hdc in next ch, sc in next ch, * ch 20, sk 1 ch, sc in next 19 ch, ch 10 and repeat from * to *, sc in next 10 ch of stem. Fasten off. Baste Stem above 1 scallop, with Shd. Pinks flower at end, Shd. Yellows flower above stem and Shd. Lavenders flower below stem, as in illustration. Sew in place. Repeat above each scallop. Steam and press dry on back thru a cloth.

Daisy Parade Pillowcase

MATERIALS REQUIRED:
DAISY Mercerized Crochet Cotton size 30.
1-skein each White and No. 10 Yellow.
Steel crochet hook No. 13.
A pair of white pillow cases.
EDGING—Flower—With White ch 11, join with sl st to form ring. *ROW 1*—Ch 1, 18 sc in ring, join with sl st to 1st sc. *ROW 2*—* Ch 1, (2 dc in next sc) twice, ch 1, sc in next sc. Repeat from * 5 times (6 petals). *ROW 3*—* Ch 23, sl st in same st, ch 3 behind next petal, sl st in next sc between petals. Repeat from * 5 times, ch 3, join to base of 1st large lp. *ROW 4*—3 hdc and 12 dc in half of next lp, * in 12th (center) ch of lp make 2 dc, ch 4, sl st in last dc for a p, and 2 dc; 12 dc and 3 hdc in bal. of lp, sl st in ch-3 behind next petal, 3 hdc and 3 dc in next lp, sl st back in 6th st up side of last petal, 5 dc back in large lp, ch 9, turn, sk next 4 dc on previous petal, sl st in next dc. Ch 1, turn, 11 sc on ch-9 lp, 4 dc up to center of large lp. Repeat from * once. (2 dc, a p and 2 dc) in center st of lp, 12 dc and 3 hdc in bal. of lp, sl st in ch-3 behind next petal, ** 3 hdc and 3 dc in next lp, sl st back in 6th st up side of last petal, 9 dc back in large lp up to center. Repeat from * to **. Fasten off. Tack 1st and 6th petals tog. by 6th st up side of each. Make 9 Flowers for each half of pillow case. Tack 1st and 6th large petals on each flower to 3d and 4th petals on next flower.

Top Edge—Join Yellow to top petal on 1 flower, * ch 7, sc in 5th ch from hook for a p, ch 9, p, ch 3, sc in center of next 11-sc, ch 7, p, ch 9, p, ch 3, tr down in joining of flowers, ch 7, p, ch 9, p, ch 3, sc in center of next 11-sc lp on next flower, ch 7, p, ch 9, p, ch 3, sc in next petal. Repeat from * around. *ROW 2*—Sl st to center of 1st p-lp, * (ch 7, p, ch 9, p, ch 3, dc in next p-lp) twice, ch 7, p, ch 9, p, ch 3, sc in next p-lp, ch 7, p, ch 11, p, ch 3, sc in next p-lp. Repeat from * around. *ROW 3*—Sl st to center of 1st p-lp, ch 12, dc in next p-lp, ch 9, dc in next p-lp, * (ch 11, dc in next p-lp) twice, (ch 9, dc in next p-lp) twice. Repeat from * around, join to 3d st of ch-12. *ROW 4*—Ch 1, sc in same st, * (9 sc in next sp, sc in next dc) twice, (11 sc in next sp, sc in next dc) twice. Repeat from * around, join and fasten off.
Bottom Edge—Join Yellow to joining of 2 flowers, * ch 12, sc in center of next 11-sc lp, ch 12, dc in next petal, ch 8, dc in same place, ch 12, sc in center of next 11-sc lp, ch 12, sc in joining of flowers. Repeat from * around. *ROW 2*—In each ch-12 lp around, make 7 sc, a 5-ch p and 7 sc. In each ch-8 lp, make 3 sc, a p, (2 sc, a p) twice, and 3 sc.
FLOWER CENTER—With Yellow, ch 2, 6 sc in 2d ch from hook, join with sl st in back lp of 1st sc. *ROW 2*—(Ch 4, sl st in same sc, sl st in next sc) 6 times. Fasten off. Sew one in center of each flower.
Sew to edge of pillow case.

Flower Edgings

(Continued from page 31)

FLOWERS—With Shd. Blue * ch 8, dc in 4th ch from hook, sk 3 ch, sl st in next ch. Ch 7, dc in 4th ch from hook, sl st in same st with sl st at base of last petal, (ch 4, dc in 4th ch from hook) twice, ch 8, dc in 4th ch from hook, sk 3 ch, sl st in next ch, (ch 4, dc in 4th ch from hook) twice. Repeat from * for about 1/3 more than desired length. Make an even no. of flowers. *ROW 2*—Working back to complete flowers, (ch 7, dc in 4th ch from hook, sl st in center st of flower) twice, * ch 4, sl st in between 2 petals between flowers inserting hook under work, not into st. Ch 4, sl st in center st of next flower, (ch 7, dc in 4th ch from hook, sl st in center st) twice, ch 4, sl st in between 2 petals between flowers, ch 4, sl st in center st of next flower, ch 7, dc in 4th ch from hook, sl st in cen-

ter st. Repeat from * across (5 petals in each flower). Fasten off. With row untwisted, join first and last flowers.
1st HEADING ROW—Join Green to 1st petal in Row 1, ch 10, dc in 2d petal of same flower, * ch 5, dtr in single free petal of next flower, ch 5, dc in 1st free petal of next flower, ** ch 7, dc in next petal. Repeat from * across, ending at ** for corner, ch 3, dc in next petal, dtr in single free petal on next flower, dc in 1st free petal on next flower ch 3, dc in next petal. Repeat from ** around, join to 3d st of ch-10. *ROW 2*—Ch 5, sk next 2 ch, dc in next 3 ch, * ch 2, dc in next dc, ch 2, dc in 3d ch of next lp, ch 2, dc in dtr, ch 2, dc in 3d ch of next lp, ch 2, dc in next dc, ** ch 2, sk 2 ch, dc in next 3 ch. Repeat from * across, ending at ** for corner, dc in corner dtr, sk next dc, dc in next ch, ch 2, dc in 3d st of next ch-5, ch 2, dc in dtr, ch 2, dc in 3d ch of next lp, ch 2, dc in next dc, ch 2, sk 2 ch, dc in next 3-

ch. Repeat from * around. Join to 3d st of ch-5. *ROW 3*—Ch 3, * 2 dc in next ch-2, dc in next dc, sk 1 dc, dc in next dc, 2 dc in next sp, dc in next dc, ** (ch 2, dc in next dc) 4 times. Repeat from * across ending at ** for corner, (ch 2, dc in next dc) 3 times, sk 3 corner dc, dc in next dc, (ch 2, dc in next dc) 3 times. Repeat from * around and join to ch-3. *ROW 4*—Ch 3, dc in next 2 dc, * ch 3, sk 3 sts, dc in next 3 dc, 2 dc in next sp, dc in dc, ** (ch 2, dc in next dc) twice, 2 dc in next sp, dc in next 3 dc. Repeat from * across, ending at ** for corner, ch 2, dc in next dc, sk 2 dc in corner, dc in next dc, ch 2, dc in next dc, 2 dc in next sp, dc in next 3 dc. Repeat from * around. Join. *ROW 5*—Ch 6, dc in next ch-3 sp, * ch 3, sk 2 dc, dc in next 4 dc, ** 2 dc in next sp, dc in dc, 2 dc in next sp, dc in 4 dc, ch 3, dc in next ch-3 sp. Repeat from * across, ending at ** for corner. Holding back

(Continued on page 45)

Rose of Summer Centerpiece

MATERIALS—DAISY Mercerized Crochet Cotton size 30:— 3 skeins or balls White, Cream or Ecru. Crochet hook size 13. Size—29 inches across points.

MOTIF—Ch 7, sl st in 1st st. Ch 7 and working over starting end of thread, make 1 dc in ring, (ch 4, dc in ring) 4 times, ch 4, sl st in 3d st of 7-ch. **ROW 2**—(Ch 1, 6 dc in next sp, ch 1, sc in next dc) 6 times. **ROW 3**—(Ch 6, sc in sc between petals) 6 times. **ROW 4**—* Ch 1, (2 dc, 5 tr and 2 dc) in next 6-ch, ch 1, sc in next sc. Repeat from * 5 times. **ROW 5**—(Ch 9, sc in sc between petals) 6 times. **ROW 6**—* Ch 1, (2 dc, 3 tr, 2 dc, ch 1, sc, ch 1, 2 dc, 3 tr and 2 dc) all in next lp, ch 1, sc in next sc. Repeat from * 5 times. **ROW 7**—Lattice Points— Sl st up to center st of next petal, (ch 17, sc in center of next petal) 11 times, ch 8, dtr in next petal. Ch 5, dc one third of way down tr, ch 2, (dc one third farther along tr and dc in 3d st of next lp) holding back the last lp of each of these 2 dc on hook, thread over and pull thru all 3 lps at once for a Cluster. * Ch 2, dc in next 3d ch st, ch 2, turn, sk last dc and Cluster, dc in next dc, ch 2, dc in 3d st of end 5-ch. Ch 5, turn, sk last dc, dc in next dc, ch 2, dc in next, ch 2, sl st in next 3d (center) st of 17-ch lp. Ch 5, dc in next 3d ch st, ch 2, (dc in next 3d ch st

and dc in 3d st of next lp) worked off tog. into a Cluster. Repeat from * around. Cut 6 inches long, thread to a needle and fasten off on back. Around this 1st (center) Motif, make and join a row of 6 Motifs, joining to each other and to center Motif by 2 Lattice Points in each joining. To join, in place of 5-ch at tip of Points in Row 7, make 2-ch, sl st in a Point on another Motif, ch 2 back and complete Point. Make and join a 2d row around of 12 Motifs, a 3d row of 18 Motifs and a 4th row of 24 Motifs (61 Motifs in all).

Edge—Join to 1st free Point on a corner Motif, ** (ch 16, sc in next Point) 5 times around same Motif, * ch 13, sc in 1st free Point on next Motif, (ch 16, sc in next Point) 3 times. Repeat from * twice. Ch 13, sc in 1st free Point on next (corner) Motif. Repeat from ** around. **ROW 2**— In each 16-ch lp, make 2 sc, 2 hdc, 7 dc, ch 5, sl st in last dc for a p, 7 dc, 2 hdc and 2 sc. In each 13-ch lp, make 2 sc, 2 hdc, 5 dc, a p, 5 dc, 2 hdc and 2 sc. Stretch and pin right-side-down in true shape. Steam and press dry thru a cloth.

34

Primrose Path

DAISY MERCERIZED CROCHET COTTON, Art. 65,
Size 30: 1 skein each White, Sal. Rose and Lt. Green.
No. 13 Steel Crochet Hook.

Rnd 1: Starting in center with White, ch 8, join with sl st to form ring. Ch 3, 23 dc in ring, join with sl st in ch-3. Ch 1 and drop but do not cut. **Rnd 2:** Attach Sal. Rose to 1 dc, (ch 1, 3 dc in next dc, ch 1, sc in next dc) 12 times. Fasten off. **Rnd 3:** Draw lp of White thru center dc of one scallop, (ch 9, sc in next scallop) 11 times, ch 4, join with tr in next scallop. **Rnd 4:** Ch 19, * long tr in 5th (center) st of next lp. To make long tr, Y O 5 times and work off in twos as for a tr. Ch 7, long tr in same st, ch 7; repeat from * around, join with ch 7, long tr at base of ch-19, ch 7, sl st in 12th st of ch-19. Fasten off. **Rnd 5:** Attach Sal. Rose to one long tr, ch 3, (7 dc in one lp of center st of next sp, dc in next long tr) 24 times, joining to top of 1st 3-ch. Fasten off. **Rnd 6:** Attach Lt. Green to center dc of one shell, ch 5, tr in same dc, * (ch 4, 2 tr) twice in same dc, 2 tr in center dc of next shell; repeat from * around, join to 1st 5-ch. Fasten off. **Rnd 7:** Attach White to 2nd ch-4 sp on one shell, ch 5, * tr in 1st sp on next shell, ch 7, sl st in one lp of 4th ch from hook for a p, ch 10, p, ch 3, tr in next sp on same shell; repeat from * around, join 24th p-lp of 1st 5-ch, sl st to center of next p-lp. **Rnd 8:** (Ch 8, p, ch 11, p, ch 4, sc in next p-lp) 24 times. Sl st to center of next p-lp. Rnd 9: (Ch 9, p, ch 12, p, ch 5, sc in next p-lp) 24 times. Fasten off. **Rnd 10: 1st CIRCLE:** With White, repeat Rnd 1. Fasten off. Attach Sal. Rose to one dc, ch 2, 2 dc in next dc, * sl st in center of one p-lp, ch 1, sl st back in last dc, complete petal with 1 dc, ch 1, sc in next dc, (ch 1, 3 dc in next dc, ch 1, sc in next dc) 11 times. Fasten off. **2d CIRCLE:** Repeat to *; sk 2d and 3d petals on 1st Circle, sl st in next (4th) petal,

ch 1, sl st back in last dc, complete petal with 1 dc, ch 1, sc in next dc, (ch 1, 3 dc in next dc, ch 1, sc in next dc) twice, ch 1, 2 dc in next dc, sl st in next p-lp to right around doily, ch 1, sl st back in last dc, complete petal with 1 dc, ch 1, sc in next dc, (ch 1, 3 dc in next dc, ch 1, sc in next dc) 8 times. Fasten off. Repeating 2d Circle, continue around doily with 22 more circles, joining to each other and to each p-lp. Join 24th Circle to 1st Circle. **Rnd 11:** Attach White to 2d petal on outside of one circle, * (ch 9, sc in next petal) twice, ch 5, dc in next petal, dc in 1st petal on next circle, ch 5, sc in next petal; repeat from * around; sl st to center of 1st lp. **Rnd 12:** (Ch 11, sc in next lp, ch 11, sc between 2 dc in angle, ch 11, sc in next ch-9 lp) repeated around, sl st to center st of 1st lp. **Rnd 13:** Ch 12, dtr in same st, (ch 5, dtr) twice in same st, * ch 5, tr in center st of next 2 lps, (ch 5, dtr) 4 times in center st of next lp; repeat from * around, join final ch-5 to 7th st of ch-12. Fasten off. **Rnd 14:** Attach Sal. Rose between 2 tr in one angle, ch 3, * dc in center st of next sp, ch 3, a 7-dc shell in one lp of center st of each of next 3 sps; ch 3, dc in center st of next sp, dc between next 2 tr in angle; repeat from * around, join to top of ch-3. Fasten off. **Rnd 15:** Attach Lt. Green to same st, ch 7, * (2 tr, ch 4, 2 tr) in center dc of next shell, 2 tr in one lp of center dc of next shell, (ch 4, 2 tr) 3 times in same dc, (2 tr, ch 4, 2 tr) in center dc of next shell, dtr in center dc in angle; repeat from * around, join to top of ch-7. Fasten off. **Rnd 16:** Attach White to dtr in one angle, * in ch-4 sp of next shell make 3 sc, ch 5, sl st in last sc for a p, 3 sc; sc between shells, (3 sc, p, 3 sc) in each of 3 sps of next shell, sc between shells, (3 sc, p, 3 sc) in next shell, sc in dtr in angle; repeat from * around, join and fasten off.

35

Flower Frills Doily

MATERIALS REQUIRED:

DAISY Mercerized Crochet Cotton size 30.

1-ball or skein White

Lily MERCROCHET Cotton size 30.

1-small ball each Dk. Yellow and Hunter Green.

Steel crochet hook No. 13.

Size—12 inches when blocked.

CENTER—1st Motif—With White ch 7, dc in 7th ch from hook, (ch 3, dc in same st) 4 times, ch 3, join with sl st in 3d st of next ch. Fasten off. ROW 2 —Join Yellow to 1 dc, ch 1, sc in same st, * ch 4, 3 tr in next sp, ch 4, sl st in last tr for a p, 3 tr in same sp with last tr, ch 4, sc in next dc. Repeat from * 5 times. Fasten off. ROW 3— Join Green to 1 s between any 2 petals, ** ch 11, * sc in 2d ch from hook, hdc in next ch, dc in next 5 ch, hdc in next ch, sl st in next ch, * ch 10 and repeat from * to *. Sk these 2 leaves, sc around next ch-1 stem, sc in same sc between petals, ch 5 back of next petal, sc in next sc between petals. Re-

peat from * 5 times (12 leaves). Fasten off. ROW 4—Join White to 1st leaf in one group of 2 leaves, * (ch 13, sc in next leaf, ch 8, sc in 1st leaf in next group) repeated around, join and fasten off.

2d Motif—Repeat to * in Row 4. Ch 6, sl st in center st of ch-13 lp on 1st Motif, ch 6, sc back in next leaf on 2d Motif, ch 4, sl st in next ch-8 lp on 1st Motif, ch 4, sc back in next leaf on 2d Motif, ch 6, sl st in center st of next ch-13 lp on 1st Motif, ch 6, sc back in next leaf on 2d Motif. Complete row as for 1st Motif.

3d Motif—Join to one side each of 1st and 2d Motifs. Make 4 more Motifs, joining to each other in a hexagon and to 1st Motif in center.

BORDER—Heading Row—Join White to center ch-8 on outside of 1 Motif, ch 14, dc in 7th (center) st of next ch-13 lp, * ch 11, tr tr in next lp, ch 5, a long tr (thread over 6 times and work off in twos) down in joining of Motifs,

ch 5, tr tr in next ch-8 lp, ch 11, dc in 7th (center) st of next lp, ch 11, dc in next lp, ch 11, dc in 7th (center) st of next lp. Repeat from * around, join to 3d st of ch-14. ROW 2—Ch 5, sk next 2 ch, dc in next st, (ch 2, sk 2 sts, dc in next st) repeated around (120 sps). Join to 3d st of ch-5. ROW 3 —* Ch 3, sk 1 dc, tr in next dc, (ch 3, tr) 3 times in same dc, ch 3, sk 1 dc, sc in next dc. Repeat from * around, join. ROW 4—Sl st to ch-3 between 1st 2 tr of next shell, ch 8, tr in next (center) sp, (ch 3, tr) 3 times in same sp, * ch 3, tr in next sp, tr in 2d ch-3 sp on next shell, (ch 3, tr) 4 times in next (center) sp. Repeat from * around, join final tr to 5th st of ch-8. ROW 5 —Repeat last row except make ch-2 between 2 tr in angle between shells. Join final ch-2 to 5th st of ch-8. ROW 6 —* (Ch 3, sk next sp, dc in next tr) twice, (ch 3, dc) twice in next (center) sp, (ch 3, dc in next tr) twice, ch 3, sc in ch-2 sp between shells. Repeat from * around, join. ROW 7—* Ch 5

(Continued on page 46)

36

Blossom Vanity Set

MATERIALS REQUIRED:
DAISY Mercerized Crochet Cotton size 20.
2-skeins White.
Steel crochet hook No. 12.

1st BLOCK — (Size—3¾ inches) — Starting in center, ch 6, join with sl st to form ring. *ROW 1*—Ch 1, 8 sc in ring, join with sl st in back lp of 1st sc. *ROW 2*—* Ch 5, 5 tr in same sc, ch 4, sl st in same sc, sl st in back lp of next 2 sc. Repeat from * 3 times. *ROW 3*—Ch 5, remove hook from lp, insert it up in center tr of next petal, catch lp and draw thru, letting ch-5 lie up back of petal. Ch 8, tr in same tr, * ch 10, dc down in center ring between petals, ch 10, (tr, ch 3, tr) in center tr on next petal. Repeat from * around, join final ch-10 with sl st in 5th st of ch-8. *ROW 4*—Sc in next (corner) ch-3 sp, ch 6, dc in same sp, (ch 3, dc) 3 times in same sp, * ch 6, dc in 6th ch of next ch-10 lp, dc in 5th ch of next ch-10 lp, ch 6, dc in ch-3 sp between next 2 tr at corner, (ch 3,

dc) 4 times in same sp. Repeat from * around, join final ch-6 to 3d ch of 1st ch-6. *ROW 5*—* Ch 10, sc in 4th ch from hook, hdc in next 2 ch, dc in next 3 ch, holding back the last lp of each dc on hook, make 2 dc in next ch, thread over and draw thru all 3 lps on hook (Cluster made), sl st in next dc. Repeat from * 3 times. 5 sc in two-thirds of next ch-6 sp, ch 11, 5 sc in left two-thirds of next ch-6 sp, sl st in next dc. Repeat from * around, join and fasten off. *ROW 6*—Join to tip of 1st point at one corner, * (ch 10, sc in next point) 3 times, ch 6, sc in next ch-11 lp, ch 6, sc in next point. Repeat from * around, join. *ROW 7*—* In each of next 3 ch-10 sps, make sc, hdc, 4 dc, ch 4, 4 dc, hdc and sc. Sc in next sc, ch 4, (tr, ch 6, tr) in sc between next 2 ch-6 sps, ch 4, sc in next sc. Repeat from * around, join and fasten off.

2d BLOCK—Repeat thru Row 6. *ROW 7*—In each of next 2 ch-10 sps, make sc, hdc, 4 dc, ch 4, 4 dc, hdc and sc.

* In half of next ch-10 sp make sc, hdc and 4 dc, ch 2, sl st in corresponding point on 1st Block, ch 2 back and make 4 dc, hdc and sc in bal. of same ch-10 sp on 2d Block, * sc in next sc, ch 4, tr in sc between next 2 ch-6 sps, ch 3, sl st in center of next corresponding shell on 1st Block, ch 3, tr back in same sc with last tr on 2d Block, ch 4, sc in next sc. Repeat from * to *. Then complete row as for 1st Block.

Join a 3d Block to 2d Block, and a 4th Block to 1st and 3d Blocks. This leave 4 points free in center opening between 4 Blocks.
FILL-IN MOTIF—Join to 1 point in opening, ch 1, sc in same place, (ch 9, sc in next point) 3 times, ch 9, join with sl st in 1st sc. Fasten off.
LARGE DOILY—Make 20 Blocks and join 4 x 5.
SMALL DOILY—(Make 2)—Make 6 Blocks and join 2 x 3.
Stretch and pin doilies right-side-down in true shape. Steam and press dry thru a cloth.

Irish Rose Doily

Approximate Size 13 inches square
This doily can be made with the following:
The Famous "PURITAN" CROCHET COTTON, Article 40
or
"DE LUXE" Quality CROCHET COTTON, Article 346
1 ball each Ecru, Pink, Nile Green or Lt. Green or colors desired
Steel crochet hook No. 7

With Pink ch 5, join to form a ring, ch 1 and work 8 s c in ring, join in 1st s c.

2nd Row—* Ch 3, s c in next s c, repeat from * all around (8 loops).

3rd Row—Ch 1 and over each loop work 1 s c, 3 d c, 1 s c, join.

4th Row—* Ch 4, sl st in back of work between next 2 petals, repeat from * 7 times.

5th Row—Ch 1 and over each loop work 1 s c, 4 d c, 1 s c, join.

6th Row—Same as 4th row but having 5 chs in each loop.

7th Row—Ch 1 and over each loop work 1 s c, 6 d c, 1 s c, join.

8th Row—Same as 4th row but having 6 chs in each loop.

9th Row—Ch 1 and over each loop work 1 s c, 8 d c, 1 s c, join.

10th Row—Same as 4th row but having 7 chs in each loop.

11th Row—Ch 1 and over each loop work 1 s c, 10 d c, 1 s c, join.

12th Row—Same as 4th row but having 8 chs in each loop.

13th Row—Ch 1 and over each loop work 1 s c, 12 d c, 1 s c, join.

14th Row—Same as 4th row but having 9 chs in each loop.

15th Row—Ch 1 and over each loop work 1 s c, 14 d c, 1 s c, join.

16th Row—Same as 4th row but having 10 chs in each loop.

17th Row—Ch 1 and over each loop work 1 s c, 3 d c, 10 tr c, 3 d c, 1 s c, join, cut thread.

LEAVES—Attach Green in 14th row in back of work between any 2 petals, ch 10, s c in 2nd st from hook, 1 s d c in each of the next 2 sts of ch (s d c: thread over hook, insert in st, pull through, thread over and pull through all loops at one time), 1 d c in each remaining st of ch, s c in same space of same row in back of work, ch 12, s c in 2nd st from hook, 1 s d c in each of the next 2 sts of ch, 1 d c in each remaining st of ch, s c in same space in back of work, ch 10 and work back on ch same as on previous ch, s c in same row in back of work, cut thread. Work another group of leaves in same manner between 3rd and 4th petals, 5th and 6th petals and 7th and 8th petals (4 groups of leaves).

Attach Ecru in tip of center leaf of any corner, * ch 6, s c in tip of next leaf, ch 6, d c in 3rd tr c of next petal, ch 6, skip 4 sts of same petal, d c in next st, ch 6, d c in 3rd tr c of next petal, ch 6, skip 4 sts of same petal, d c in next st, ch 6, s c in tip of 1st leaf of corner, ch 6, s c in tip of next leaf, repeat from * all around.

2nd Row—Ch 1, s c in same space, ** 5 s c in next loop, s c in next s c, * 5 s c in next loop, s c in next d c, repeat from * 3 times, * 5 s c in next loop, s c in next s c, repeat from * once, repeat from ** all around ending to correspond, join.

3rd Row—Ch 10, d c in same space, * ch 1, skip 1 s c, d c in next s c, repeat from * all around working 1 d c, ch 7, 1 d c in center st at each corner (21 meshes on each side not counting corners), ch 1, join in 3rd st of ch.

4th Row—Sl st into loop, ch 5, tr c in same space, * ch 1, tr c in same space, repeat from * 5 times, ** skip 1 mesh, 3 d c in next mesh, * ch 1, skip 1 mesh, 3 d c in next mesh, repeat from * 8 times, skip 1 mesh, 8 tr c with ch 1 between each tr c in corner loop, repeat from ** all around ending to correspond, join in 4th st of ch.

5th Row—Ch 5, tr c in same space, * ch 1, 1 tr c, ch 1, 1 tr c in next tr c, repeat from * 6 times, skip 3 d c, 3 d c in next ch 1 space, * ch 1, 3 d c in next ch 1 space, repeat from * 7 times, skip 3 d c, 1 tr c, ch 1, 1 tr c in next tr c, repeat from 1st * all around ending to correspond, join in 4th st of ch.

6th Row—Ch 6, tr c in next tr c, * ch 2, tr c in next tr c, repeat from * 13 times, ** skip 3 d c, 3 d c in next ch 1 space, * ch 1, 3 d c in next ch 1 space, repeat from * 6 times, tr c in next tr c, * ch 2, tr c in next tr c, repeat from * 14 times, repeat from ** all around ending to correspond, join in 4th st of ch.

7th Row—Ch 7 and work same as last row but having 3 chs between each tr c around corners and having 7 groups of d c on each side.

8th Row—Ch 8 and work same as last row but having 4 chs between each tr c and having 6 groups of d c on each side.

Work 5 more rows in same manner starting each row with 1 more ch and

(Continued on page 46)

Blossom Doily

Approximate Size 12½ inches in diameter
This doily can be made with the following:
The Famous "PURITAN" CROCHET COTTON, Article 40
or
"DE LUXE" Quality CROCHET COTTON, Article 346
1 ball each White, Kelly Green and Shaded Yellows
or colors desired
Steel crochet hook No. 7

With Shaded Yellows ch 9, join to form a ring, ch 4, 2 tr c in ring keeping last loop of each st on hook, thread over and work off all loops at one time, * ch 5, cluster st in same space (cluster st: 3 tr c in same space keeping last loop of each st on hook, thread over and work off all loops at one time), repeat from * 6 times, ch 5, join in top of 1st cluster st, cut thread.

2nd Round—Attach Green in any loop, ch 1 and work 3 s c, ch 3, 3 s c in each loop, join in 1st s c.

3rd Round—Sl st to ch 3 loop, ch 4 (always counts as part of 1st cluster st), 2 tr c in same space keeping last loop of each st on hook, thread over and work off all loops at one time, ch 5, cluster st in same space, ch 7, 2 cluster sts with ch 5 between in next ch 3 loop, repeat from * all around, ch 7, join in 1st cluster st.

4th Round—Attach White in any ch 5 loop, s c in same space, * ch 7, s c in next loop, ch 7, s c in next loop, ch 7, s c in same loop, repeat from * all around ending with ch 3, tr c in 1st s c (this brings thread in position for next round).

5th Round—2 s c over tr c, * ch 5, 2 s c in next loop, repeat from * all around ending with ch 1, tr c in 1st s c.

6th Round—2 s c over tr c, ch 6, 2 s c in next loop, repeat from * all around ending with ch 2, tr c in 1st s c.

7th Round—2 s c over tr c, * ch 7, 2 s c in next loop, repeat from * all around ending with ch 3, tr c in 1st s c.

8th Round—2 s c over tr c, * ch 8, 2 s c in next loop, repeat from * all around ending with ch 3, d tr c in 1st s c.

9th Round—* Ch 9, s c in next loop, repeat from * all around, ch 9, join in d tr c, cut thread.

10th Round—Attach Green in any loop, ch 1 and work 5 s c, ch 3, 5 s c in each loop, join in 1st s c.

11th Round—Attach Shaded Yellows in any ch 3 loop, ch 4, cluster st in same space, * ch 4, cluster st in same space, repeat from * once, cut thread. * Skip two - ch 3 loops, attach Shaded Yellows in next loop, ch 4, cluster st in same loop, ch 4, cluster st in same space, ch 4, cluster st in same space, cut thread, repeat from * 6 times.

12th Round—Attach Green in 1st ch 3 loop after any cluster st group, s c in same space, * ch 8, s c in next ch 3 loop, ch 7, 5 s c in next loop between cluster sts, ch 3, 5 s c in next loop, ch 7, s c in next ch 3 loop, repeat from * all around ending to correspond, join in 1st s c.

13th Round—* 5 s c in next loop, ch 3, 5 s c in same loop, 4 s c, ch 3, 4 s c in next loop, ch 5, 1 s c, ch 3, 1 s c in next ch 3 loop, ch 5, 4 s c, ch 3, 4 s c in next loop, repeat from * all around ending to correspond, join, cut thread.

14th Round—Attach White in any ch 3 loop above cluster st group, s c in same space, ch 5, s c in next loop, ch 5, s c in next loop, ch 7, s c in next loop, ch 7, s c in next loop, * ch 5, s c in next loop, repeat from * 3 times, ch 7, s c in next loop, ch 7, s c in next loop, repeat from 1st * 6 times, ch 5, s c in next loop, ch 1, tr c in 1st s c.
Repeat the 6th, 7th and 8th rounds once.

18th Round—2 s c over d tr c, * ch 9, 2 s c in next loop, repeat from * all around ending with ch 4, d tr c in 1st s c.

19th and 20th Rounds—Same as 9th and 10th rounds.

21st Round—Attach Shaded Yellows in any ch 3 loop directly above the group of Shaded Yellow cluster sts of previous round and work in same manner as 11th round, but repeat from * 14 times.

22nd Round—Same as 12th round.

23rd Round—Same as 13th round.

Rose Filet Pillow

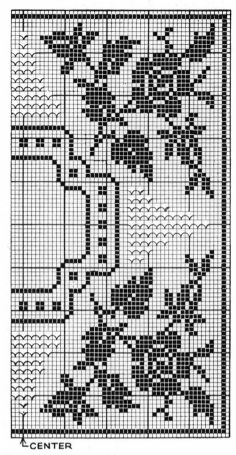

There are 10 spaces between heavy lines

MATERIALS:

J. & P. COATS or **CLARK'S O.N.T. BEST SIX CORD MERCERIZED CROCHET,** *Size 30:*

SMALL BALL:

J. & P. COATS —6 balls of White or Ecru, or 8 balls of any color,

or

CLARK'S O.N.T.—8 balls of White or Ecru, or 9 balls of any color.

BIG BALL:

J. & P. COATS —3 balls of White, Ecru or Cream.

Steel Crochet Hook No. 10 or 11.

A ruffled pillow 20 inches square (excluding ruffle).

GAUGE: 5 sps measure 1 inch; 5 rows measure 1 inch.

Starting at bottom of chart, make a chain about 25 inches long (15 ch sts to 1 inch). **1st row:** Dc in 8th ch from hook, * ch 2, skip 2 ch, dc in next ch (2 sps are made). Repeat from * until 100 sps in all are made. Cut off remaining chain. Ch 5, turn. **2nd row:** Dc in next dc, * 2 dc in next sp, dc in next dc (bl over sp is made). Repeat from * across to within last sp, ch 2, dc in center st of turning ch. Ch 5, turn. **3rd row:** Dc in next dc, dc in next 3 dc (bl over bl is made); * ch 2, skip 2 dc, dc in next dc (sp over bl is made). Repeat from * across to within last bl, make bl over bl, sp over last sp. Ch 5, turn. **4th row:** 1 sp, 1 bl, 2 sps, 1 bl, 31 sps, 1 bl, 26 sps, 1 bl, 31 sps, 1 bl, 2 sps, 1 bl, 1 sp. Ch 5, turn.

Note: Chart shows slightly more than one half of the design (exact center is marked with an arrow). Follow chart to center. For second half of each row, repeat the first half, starting at center and working back.

5th row: Follow chart. Ch 5, turn. **6th row:** 1 sp, 1 bl, 2 sps, 2 bls, 2 sps, 1 bl, 6 sps, 1 bl, 2 sps, 1 bl, 13 sps, 3 bls, 1 sp, 2 bls, 2 sps, 3 bls, 6 sps; ch 3, sc in next dc, ch 3, dc in next dc (lacet is made), 6 sps, 3 bls, 2 sps, 2 bls, 1 sp, 3 bls, 13 sps, 1 bl, 2 sps, 1 bl, 6 sps, 1 bl, 2 sps, 2 bls, 2 sps, 1 bl, 1 sp. Ch 5, turn. **7th row:** Follow chart across to within lacet, ch 5, dc in next dc (bar is made), 3 sps, 9 bls, 1 sp, 3 bls, 6 sps, 2 bls, 7 sps, 2 bls, 7 sps, 5 bls, 2 sps, 1 bl, 1 sp. Ch 5, turn. **8th row:** Follow chart across to bar, ch 3, skip 2 ch, sc in next ch, ch 3, dc in next dc (lacet made), 4 sps, 2 bls, 4 sps, 2 bls, 1 sp, 2 bls, 4 sps, 1 bl, 1 sp, 6 bls, 6 sps, 1 bl, 6 sps, 5 bls, 2 sps, 1 bl, 1 sp. Ch 5, turn. **9th row:** Follow chart across. **10th row:** Follow chart to within 2 sps preceding bar, make a lacet as in 6th row. Make a lacet as in 8th row. Make another lacet as in 6th row. 4 sps, 7 bls, 5 sps, 5 bls, 10 sps, 1 bl, 4 sps, 6 bls, 3 sps, 1 bl, 1 sp. Ch 5, turn. Now follow chart as before, until 25th row is completed. **26th row:** Follow chart across making 2 ch-2 sps over each bar. Ch 5, turn. Work in this manner, following chart to top. Then work a row of sc closely all around. Fasten off.

Pin crocheted piece into shape and press with hot iron through damp cloth. Sew onto pillow.

Spring Garden Luncheon Set

MATERIALS—DAISY Mercerized Crochet Cotton size 30—3 skeins or balls White (sufficient for 4 Place Mats 11½x18 inches and 4 Glass Doilies 5 inches). Crochet hook size 12 or 13. 30-inch piece of 36-inch linen in desired color.

FLOWER—Ch 7, dc in 1st st, (ch 3, dc in same st) 4 times, ch 3, sl st in 3d st of next 6-ch. **ROW 2**—(Ch 1, 4 dc in next sp, ch 1, sc in next dc) 6 times. **ROW 3**—* Ch 7, 2 tr in 6th ch st from hook, holding back the last lp of each tr, thread over and pull thru all 3 lps on hook at once (a Cluster made), ch 4, sl st in top Cluster for a p, ch 6, sl st at base of Cluster, ch 1, sl st in back lp of sc between next 2 petals. Repeat from * 5 times. **ROW 4**—Ch 3 for a dc, * ch 6, (dc, ch 6, dc) in p at top of next Cluster, ch 6, dc in same st where

sl st was made between next 2 petals. Repeat from * around. Join final 6-ch with sl st in 3d st of 1st 9-ch lp. **ROW 5**—(2 sc, 1 hdc and 4 dc) in next 6-ch, * dc in dc, (5 dc, a 4-ch p and 5 dc) in next 6-ch, dc in dc, (4 dc, 1 hdc and 2 sc) in next **sp,** (2 sc, 1 hdc and 1 dc) in next sp, remove hook, insert it back in 4th st up side of last petal, catch lp and pull thru, 3 dc in bal. of sp. Repeat from * around. Sl st in 1st 4 sts and fasten to last petal with sl st. Cut 6 inches long, thread to a needle and fasten off on back.

No. 1 LEAF—Ch 31, dc in 7th st from hook, (ch 2, tr in next 3d ch st) twice, (ch 2, dtr in next 3d st) 3 times, ch 2, tr in next 3d st, ch 2, dc in next 3d st, ch 2, sl st in next 3d (end) st, ch 5, dc in next 3d st on

(Continued on page 46)

Lily of the Valley

Materials Required: AMERICAN THREAD COMPANY The Famous "PURITAN" MERCERIZED CROCHET COTTON, Article 40

2 balls White, Cream or Ecru
Approximate size of doily: 21 inches in diameter or

The Famous "PURITAN" STAR SPANGLED MERCERIZED CROCHET COTTON, Article 40

5 balls Silver Spangle or color of your choice.
Approximate size of doily: 25 inches in diameter.
Steel crochet hook No. 7

Chain (ch) 6, join to form a ring, ch 6, double crochet (d c) in ring, * ch 3, d c in ring, repeat from * 5 times, ch 3, join in 3rd stitch (st) of ch.

2nd Round. Slip stitch (sl st) into loop, ch 4 (counts as 1 treble crochet [tr c]), 4 tr c in same space keeping last loop of each st on hook, thread over and pull through all loops at one time, * ch 5, 5 tr c cluster st in next loop (5 tr c cluster st: 5 tr c in same space keeping last loop of each st on hook, thread over and pull through all loops at one time), repeat from * 6 times, ch 5, join in top of 1st cluster st.

3rd Round. Sl st into loop, ch 4, 2 trc, ch 2, 3 tr c in same space, * ch 3, 3 tr c, ch 2, 3 tr c in next loop, repeat from * 6 times, ch 3, join in 4th st of ch.

4th Round. Ch 4, tr c in same space, 1 tr c in each of the next 2 tr c, * ch 2, 1 tr c in each of the next 2 tr c, 2 tr c in next tr c, ch 3, 2 tr c in next tr c, 1 tr c in each of the next 2 tr c, repeat from * all around ending to correspond, ch 3, join.

5th Round. Ch 4, tr c in same space, 1 tr c in each of the next 3 tr c, * ch 2, 1 tr c in each of the next 3 tr c, 2 tr c in next tr c, ch 4, 2 tr c in next tr c, 1 tr c in each of the next 3 tr c, repeat from * all around ending to correspond, ch 4, join.

6th Round. Ch 4, 1 tr c in each of the next 4 tr c, * ch 2, 1 tr c in each of the next 5 tr c, ch 2, tr c in next loop, ch 4, 1 tr c in each of the next 5 tr c, repeat from * all around ending with ch 2, tr c in next loop, ch 4, join.

7th Round. Ch 4, 1 tr c in each of the next 4 tr c, * ch 2, 1 tr c in each of the next 3 tr c, 2 tr c cluster over next 2 sts (2 tr c cluster: 1 tr c in each of the next 2 sts keeping last loop of each st on hook, thread over and work off all loops at one time), ch 3, skip the next loop, tr c in next loop, ch 4, 2 tr c in next tr c, ch 4, 1 tr c in same space as last st worked in and in next tr c keeping last loop of each st on hook, thread over and work off all loops at one time, 1 tr c in each of the next 3 tr c, repeat from * 6 times, ch 2, 1 tr c in each of the next 3 tr c, 2 tr c cluster over next 2 tr c, ch 3, skip next loop, tr c in next loop, ch 4, 2 tr c in same space with ch 4, ch 4, join in 1st tr c.

8th Round. Ch 4, 1 tr c in each of the next 3 tr c, * skip next loop, 1 tr c in each of the next 2 tr c, 2 tr c cluster over next 2 sts, ch 4, skip next loop, tr c in next loop, ch 4, 1 tr c in each of the next 2 tr c, ch 4, tr c in next loop, ch 4, 2 tr c cluster over next 2 sts, 1 tr c in each of the next 2 tr c, repeat from * all around to correspond, join in 1st tr c.

9th Round. Ch 4, 1 tr c in each of the next 3 tr c, 2 tr c cluster over next 2 sts, * ch 4, tr c in next loop, repeat from * once, ch 3, 1 tr c in each of the next 2 tr c, ch 2, 2 tr c, ch 1, 2 tr c in same space as last st worked in, ch 3, skip next loop, tr c in next loop, ch 4, 2 tr c cluster over next 2 sts, 1 tr c in each of the next 2 tr c, 2 tr c cluster

over next 2 sts, repeat from 1st * all around ending to correspond, join in 1st tr c.

10th Round. Ch 4, 1 tr c in each of the next 3 sts keeping last loop of each st on hook, thread over and pull through all loops at one time, * ch 4, tr c in next loop, repeat from * once, ch 3, skip next loop, 1 tr c in each of the next 2 tr c, ch 4, 2 tr c in next tr c, tr c in next tr c, ch 2, tr c in next tr c, 2 tr c in next tr c, ch 3, skip next loop, tr c in next loop, ch 4, 1 tr c in each of the next 4 sts keeping last loop of each st on hook, thread over and work off all loops at one time, repeat from 1st * all around ending to correspond, join in 1st tr c.

11th Round. Ch 8, * tr c in next loop, ch 5, 6 tr c cluster st in next loop (6 tr c cluster st: 6 tr c in same space keeping last loop of each st on hook, thread over and work off all loops at one time), skip next loop, 1 tr c in each of the next 2 tr c, ch 4, tr c in next loop, ch 4, 2 tr c in next tr c, 1 tr c in each of the next 2 tr c, ch 2, 1 tr c in each of the next 2 tr c, 2 trc in next tr c, ch 3, skip next loop, tr c in next loop, ch 4, tr c in top of next cluster st, ch 4, repeat from * all around ending to correspond, join in 4th st of ch.

12th Round. Sl st into loop, ch 8, tr c in next loop, ** ch 3, 1 tr c in each of the next 2 tr c, * ch 4, tr c in next loop, repeat from * once, ch 2, 2 tr c, ch 4, 2 tr c in next tr c, 1 tr c in each of the next 3 tr c, ch 2, 1 tr c in each of the next 3 tr c, 2 tr c in next tr c, ch 4, skip next loop, tr c in next loop, * ch 4, tr c in next loop, repeat from * once, then repeat from ** all around ending to correspond, join in 4th st of ch.

13th Round. Ch 4 (counts as 1st tr c) and complete a 6 tr c cluster st in same loop, ** skip next loop, 1 tr c in each of the next 2 tr c, * ch 4, tr c in next loop, repeat from * once, ch 3, skip next loop, 1 tr c in each of the next 2 tr c, ch 4, tr c in next loop, ch 4, 2 tr c cluster st over next 2 tr c, 1 tr c in each of the next 3 tr c, ch 2, 1 tr c in each of the next 3 tr c, 2 tr c cluster st over next 2 tr c, * ch 4, tr c in next loop, repeat from * once, ch 5, 6 tr c cluster st in next loop, repeat from ** all around ending to correspond, join in 1st tr c.

14th Round. Ch 4, tr c in next tr c, ** ch 4, tr c in next loop, ch 5, 6 tr c cluster st in next loop, skip next loop, 1 tr c in each of the next 2 tr c, * ch 4, tr c in next loop, repeat from * once, ch 4, 2 tr c cluster over next 2 sts, tr c in next tr c, 2 tr c in next tr c, ch 1, 2 tr c in next tr c, tr c in next tr c, 2 tr c cluster over next 2 sts, * ch 4, tr c in next loop, repeat from * twice, ch 3, 1 tr c in each of the next 2 tr c, repeat from ** all around ending to correspond, join in 4th st of ch.

15th Round. Ch 4, tr c in next tr c, * ch 4, tr c in next loop, repeat from * once, ch 3, 1 tr c in each of the next 2 tr c, * ch 4, tr c in next loop, repeat from * twice, ch 4, 2 tr c cluster over next 2 sts, 1 tr c in each of the next 2 sts, skip next ch 1 space, 1 tr c in each of the next 2 tr c, 2 tr c cluster over next 2 sts, * ch 4, tr c in next loop, repeat from * once, ch 5, 6 tr c cluster st in next loop, skip next loop, 1 tr c in each of the next 2 tr c, repeat from 1st * all around ending to correspond, join.

16th Round. Ch 4, tr c in next tr c, * ch 5, tr c in next loop, ch 5, 6 tr c cluster st in next loop, skip next loop, 1 tr c in each of the next 2 tr c, * ch 4, tr c in next loop, repeat from * 3 times, ch 4, 2 tr c cluster over next 2 sts, 1 tr c in each of the next 2 sts, 2 tr c cluster over next 2 sts,

* ch 4, tr c in next loop, repeat from * twice, ch 3, 1 tr c in each of the next 2 sts, repeat from 1st * all around ending to correspond, join.

17th Round. Ch 4, tr c in next tr c, * ch 4, tr c in next loop, repeat from * once, ch 3, 1 tr c in each of the next 2 tr c,* ch 4, tr c in next loop, repeat from * 4 times, ch 4, 4 tr c cluster over next 4 sts, * ch 4, tr c in next loop, repeat from * once, ch 5, 6 tr c cluster st in next loop, skip next loop, 2 tr c cluster over next 2 sts, repeat from 1st * all around ending to correspond, join in 1st tr c.

18th Round. Ch 8, tr c in next loop, * ch 5, 6 tr c cluster st in next loop, skip next loop, 2 tr c cluster over next 2 sts, * ch 4, tr c in next loop, repeat from * 8 times, ch 4, tr c in next cluster st, ch 4, tr c in next loop, repeat from 1st * all around ending to correspond, join.

19th Round. Sl st to center of loop, ch 8, tr c in next loop, ** ch 4, tr c in next cluster st, * ch 4, tr c in next loop, repeat from * 11 times, repeat from ** all around ending to correspond, join.

20th Round. Sl st to center of loop, ch 9, tr c in next loop, * ch 5, tr c in next loop, repeat from * 3 times, ** ch 5, 6 tr c cluster st in next loop, * ch 5, tr c in next loop, repeat from * 11 times, repeat from ** all around, ending to correspond, join.

21st Round. Sl st to center of loop, ch 9, tr c in next loop, * ch 5, tr c in next loop, repeat from * once, ** ch 5, 6 tr c cluster st in next loop, ch 5, 6 tr c cluster st in next loop, ch 3, 3 double treble crochet (d tr c [3 times over hook]) with ch 3 between each d tr c in next cluster st, ch 3, 6 tr c cluster st in next loop, ch 5, 6 tr c cluster st in next loop, * ch 5, tr c in next loop, repeat from * 8 times, repeat from ** all around ending to correspond, join.

22nd Round. Sl st to center of loop, ch 9, tr c in next loop, ** ch 5, 6 tr c cluster st in next loop, ch 5, 6 tr c cluster st in next loop, * ch 5, tr c in next loop, repeat from * twice, ch 5, d tr c in next d tr c, * ch 5, tr c in next loop, repeat from * twice, ch 5, 6 tr c cluster st in next loop,

(Continued on page 46)

Pretty Daisy Doily

MATERIALS — DAISY Mercerized Crochet Cotton size 30:—1-ball each White and Lt. Blue. 1-skein Lily Six Strand Floss in Orange. Crochet hook size 13. Size—12".

CENTER—In White, ch 7, sl st in 1st st. Ch 3, 15 dc in ring, sl st in 1st ch-3. **ROW 2**—Ch 3, dc in same st, (ch 3, sk 1 dc, 2 dc in next dc) 7 times, ch 3, sl st in 1st ch-3. **ROW 3**—Ch 3, dc in same st, 2 dc in next dc, * ch 4, (2 dc in next dc) twice. Repeat from * around. Ch 4, sl st in 1st ch-3. **ROW 4**—Ch 3, dc in same st, (dc in each dc across group with 2 dc in end dc, ch 4, 2 dc in 1st dc in next group) repeated around and join (6 dc in each group). Repeat Row 4 twice (10 dc in each group in final row). **ROW 7**—Ch 3, dc in same st, 2 dc in next dc, (1 dc in each dc across group with 2 dc in each dc across group with 2 dc in each of 2 end dc, ch 3, 2 dc in each of 1st 2 dc in next group) repeated around and join to 1st ch-3 (14 dc in each group). **ROW 8** —Repeat last row but with only ch-2 between groups (18 dc in each group). **ROW 9**—Repeat Row 7 but with only ch-1 between groups (22 dc in each group). **ROW 10**—Ch 3, dc in each dc around with 1 dc between groups. **ROW 11**—Ch 3, dc in next 21 dc, * (dc, ch 12, dc) in next dc between groups, dc in next 22 dc. Repeat from * around. Sl st in 1st ch-3. **ROW 12**—Ch 3, dc in next 21 dc, * sk 1 dc, 7 sc across center of next ch-12 lp, sk 1 dc, dc in next 22 dc. Repeat from * around.

After final 7 sc, sl st in 1st ch-3. **ROW 13** — Ch 3, dc in next 19 dc, * holding back the last lp of each dc on hook, make dc in next 2 dc, thread over and pull thru all lps on hook (a Cluster made). Ch 20, (dc in 1st 2 dc in next group) made into a Cluster, dc in next 18 dc. Repeat from * around. End with ch-20, sk 1st ch-3, sl st in next dc. **ROW 14**—Ch 3, * (dc in next 2 dc) made into a Cluster, dc in next 14 dc, (dc in next 2 dc) made into a Cluster, 17 sc across center of next ch-20, sk 1st dc in next group and repeat from * around. End with sl st in 1st Cluster. **ROW 15**—Ch 3, (dc in next 2 dc) made into a Cluster, * dc in next 3 dc, (dc in next 3 dc) made into a Cluster, dc in next 4 dc, (dc in next 3 dc) made into a Cluster, ch 11, dtr in 3d sc on next lp, (ch 8, sk 3 sc, dtr in next sc) 3 times, ch 11, (dc in 1st 3 dc in next group) made into a Cluster. Repeat from * around, ending with ch 11, sl st in 1st Cluster. **ROW 16**— Repeat last row to *. * Dc in next dc, (dc in next 2 dc) made into a Cluster, dc in next dc, (dc in next 3 dc) made into a Cluster, sk 1st 3 sts of next ch-11, 10 sc over bal. of lp, sc in dtr, (9 sc in next ch-8 lp, sc in dtr) 3 times, 10 sc in next lp, sk 1st dc in next group, (dc in next 2 dc) made into a Cluster. Repeat from * around. Sl st in 1st Cluster. **ROW 17**—Ch 3, (dc in next 4 dc) made into a Cluster, * ch

13, sk 10 sc, tr in next sc, (ch 13. sk 9 sc, dtr in next sc) twice, ch 13, sk 9 sc, tr in next sc, ch 13, (dc in next 5 dc) made into a Cluster. Repeat from * around. Sl st in 1st Cluster. **ROW 18**—Ch 2, * sk 3 sts of next lp, 12 sc over bal. of lp, (15 sc in next lp) 3 times, 12 sc in next lp. Repeat from * around. Sl st in 1st sc. Fasten off.

To join Flower Row to edge of Center, work around from left to right:— **FLOWER**—In Blue, ch 7, sl st in 1st st. (ch 11, sk 3 ch, 2 dc, 5 tr and 1 dc in bal. of ch, sc in ring) 4 times. Join to Center by next 2 petals:—Ch 9, sl st in center of 1st sp on one scallop of last row, sk last st of ch-9, (2 dc, 5 tr and 1 dc) in bal. of ch, sc in ring. Join next petal in same way to 1st sp up side of next scallop to right around edge. Fasten off. **2d FLOWER**—Make 3 petals, then join 4th petal to right-hand side petal of last Flower, * join 5th petal to center of next sp to right around edge, and join 6th petal to 5th sc in next (center) sp to right around edge. **3d FLOWER** —Repeat 2d Flower to *. Join 5th petal to next 6th sc on same center sp, and join 6th petal to center sc on next sp to right around edge. **4th FLOWER**—Repeat 2d Flower to *. Join 5th petal to center of next (end) sp on same scallop, and join 6th petal to center of 1st

(Continued on page 45)

44

Pretty Daisy Doily

(Continued from page 44)

sp on next scallop. Repeat 2d, 3d and 4th FLOWERS around doily (24 Flowers).

EDGE—Sc in White in 1st of 2 outside petals on one flower, (ch 15, sc in next petal of same flower, ch 15, sc in 1st petal on next flower) repeated around. End with ch 8, dtr in 1st sc. **ROW 2—*** Ch 6, tr tr in center st of next lp, (ch 6, sc in 5th ch from hook for a p, ch 2, tr tr in same st with last tr tr) 6 times, ch 6, sc in next lp. Repeat from * around. **Fasten off.**

In Orange Floss, make 6 large French Knots in center of each Flower. Stretch and pin doily right-side-down in a true circle. Steam and press dry thru a cloth.

Flower Edgings

(Continued from page 33)

the last lp of each dc on hook, make (2 dc in next sp, dc between corner dc 2 dc in next sp) thread over and draw thru all lps on hook (Cluster made), dc in next 4 dc, ch 3, dc in next ch-3 sp. Repeat from * around. Join. *ROW 6—*Ch 1, sc in next sp, ch 6, dc in next sp, * ch 4, sk 3 dc, dc in next 7 dc, ch 4, dc in next sp, ch 3, dc in next sp. Repeat from * across, ch 3, dc in corner Cluster, (ch 3, dc in next sp) twice. Repeat from * around. Join. Fasten off.

With 3 threads Dk. Yellow Floss make a French Knot in center of each flower, carrying it along on back of petals between flowers.

Stretch and pin Edging right-side-down. Steam and press dry thru a cloth.

NO. 10—VIOLET EDGING

(Illustrated Page 31, lower center)

*MATERIALS—*Lily Mercrochet Cotton size 30 in Blue and Hunter Green. (DAISY Mercerized Crochet Cotton may be substituted if preferred). Lily Six Strand Floss in Dk. Yellow. Crochet hook No. 13. Size—2 inches.

*1st VIOLET—*With Blue ch 14, ** holding back the last lp of each dtr on hook, make 4 dtr in 8th ch from hook, thread over and draw thru all lps on hook (Cluster made). Ch 9, a 3-dtr Cluster in 8th ch from hook, ch 3, sl st in tip of Cluster (picot made), ch 7, sl st down in same place as Cluster was made (petal completed), sl st in next ch, * ch 8, a 3-dtr Cluster in 8th ch from hook, a ch-3 p, ch 7, sl st down in same place as Cluster was made, sl st in same ch between 1st 2 petals. Repeat from * once. *5th Petal—*Ch 8, a 4-dtr Cluster in 8th ch from hook.

*2d VIOLET—*Ch 19 and repeat from ** for desired length. Ch 5 and fasten off.

*1st HEADING ROW—*Join Green to last ch, ch 6, sk 1 ch, tr in next ch, * ch 7, sk 1 ch, a 2-dtr Cluster in next ch, ch 2, sk 2 petals, a 2-dtr Cluster in 1st ch of next ch-11 lp, ch 7, sk 1 ch, tr in next ch, (ch 1, sk 1 ch, tr in next ch) 3 times. Repeat from * across Fasten off. *ROW 2—*Join to 5th st of 1st ch-6 in last row, ch 6, tr in next tr, * (ch 1, sk 1 ch, tr in next ch) twice, ch 4, tr between next 2 Clusters, ch 4, sk Cluster, tr in 4th st of next ch-7, ch 1, sk 1 ch, tr in next ch, (ch 1, tr in next tr) 4 times. Repeat from * across. Fasten off.

*EDGE—*Join Green to end of Violet Row, ch 12, sc in 1st free petal of next Violet, * ch 9, (dc, ch 9, dc) in next petal, ch 9, sc in next petal, ch 5, dtr in center ch between flowers, ch 5, sc in 1st free petal on next Violet. Repeat from * across. Fasten off. *ROW 2—*Sk 1st ch-12 lp in last row, join Green and make * 10 sc in next ch-9 lp, hdc and 5 dc in half of next lp, ch 6, sl st in 5th ch from hook for a p, ch 2, 5 dc and hdc in same lp, 10 sc in next lp, sc in next ch-5 lp, ch 7, sc in left end of next ch-5 lp. Repeat from * across. Fasten off. With 3 threads of Dk. Yellow Floss, make a French Knot in center of each Violet. Stretch and pin Edging right-side-down. Steam and press dry thru a cloth.

NO. 11—BEGONIA EDGING

(Illustrated Page 31, upper left)

*MATERIALS—*Lily Mercrochet Cotton size 20 in Shd. Pinks and Bright Nile Green (DAISY Mercerized Crochet Cotton may be substituted if preferred). Crochet hook No. 12. Size—1¾ inches.
*FLOWER—*With Shd. Pinks * ch 13, holding back the last lp of each tr on hook, make 3 tr in 6th ch from hook, thread over and draw thru all lps (Cluster made), sk next 6 ch, sl st in next ch drawn tight (one petal made). Repeat from * 4 times, sc at base of center petal, sk next petal, sl st at base of next (1st) petal. Fasten off on back. Make flowers for desired length, spaced ¼ inch apart. Place flowers in Edging so 1st and 5th petals are at top.
*HEADING ROW—*Join Green to tip of 5th petal on one flower, * ch 4, tr between petals into center of flower, ch 4, sc in next (1st) petal, ch 9, sc in 5th petal of another flower. Repeat from * around. At corners, omit ch-9 between 3 flowers. Join row to 1st sc. *ROW 2—** Ch 6, 4 dc in next tr, ch 6, 2 sc in next ch-9 lp. Repeat from * around. At corners, make ch 5, sc in corner tr, ch 5, 3 dc in next tr. Join row. *ROW 3—*Ch 3, * 6 dc in next ch-6, dc in next 4 dc, 6 dc in next ch-6, dc in next 2 sc. Repeat from * around. At corners, make 3 dc in 1st ch-5, (dc in same sp, dc in next sc, dc in next sp) made into a Cluster, 3 dc in bal. of sp, dc in next 4 dc. Join row. Fasten off.
*EDGE—*Join Green to 1st free petal on a corner flower, * (ch 9, sc in next petal) twice, dtr down in next petal of same flower where sc in Heading Row was worked, dtr in corresponding petal on next flower, sc in next free petal. Repeat from * around. Join. *ROW*

2—* 10 sc in next ch-9 lp, sc in next sc, ch 5, sl st in last sc for a p, 4 sc in next lp, ch 12, turn, sl st in 4th sc to left of p, ch 1, turn, (7 sc, a p, 3 sc) in ¾'s of lp, ch 10, turn, sl st in 3d sc on left of p, ch 1, turn, (6 sc, p, 5 sc, sl st) in lp, ch 1, 3 sc and sl st in bal. of next lp, ch 1, 6 sc in bal. of next lp, sc between next 2 dtr. Repeat from * around. Fasten off.
Stretch and pin Edging right-side-down in true shape. Steam and press dry thru a cloth.

NO. 12—FUCHSIA EDGING

(Illustrated Page 31, lower left)

*MATERIALS—*Lily Mercrochet Cotton size 20 in Beauty Pink, Beauty Rose and Bright Nile Green. (DAISY Mercerized Crochet Cotton may be substituted if preferred). Crochet hook No. 12. Size—2 inches.

*BRAID—*With Green ch 9, 6 tr in 9th ch from hook. *ROW 2—*Ch 7, turn, tr in 2d tr, (ch 1, sk 1 tr, tr in next tr) twice, ch 4, 6 tr in end ch-8. *ROW 3—*Ch 7, turn, tr in 2d tr, (ch 1, sk 1 tr, tr in next tr) twice, ch 4, 6 tr in next ch-4 sp. Repeat Row 3 for desired length.

HEADING ROW—(Ch 11, sc in next point) repeated across top. End with ch 15, sc in end of Braid.

*1st EDGE ROW—*Ch 15, sc in next point on other side of Braid, * (ch 5, sc) 3 times in same point, ch 8, sc in next point. Repeat from * across. Fasten off.

*FUCHSIAS—*Join Pink to center p of 1st p-group, * ch 5, 5 tr in same p. Ch 3, turn, holding back the last lp of each tr on hook, make dc in 1st 2 tr, thread over and draw thru all lps on hook (Cluster made), (dc in next 2 sts made into a Cluster) twice, cut 1½ inches long and pull thru lp tightly. Turn and join Pink to center p in next group. Repeat from * across. *ROW 2—*Join Rose to 1st flower. Hold end of Pink across top of flower and working over it, ch 3, dc in same st, * ch 3, sc in same st, hdc and dc in next Cluster, ch 3, sl st in dc for a p, dc and hdc in same Cluster, sc in next Cluster, ch 3, a 2-dc Cluster in same st (Fuchsia completed). Cut remaining end of Pink close to work. Hold next Pink end across top of flower and working over it, make a 2-dc Cluster in 1st st on next flower. Repeat from * across. Fasten off.
Stretch and pin Edging right-side-down in true shape. Steam and press dry thru a cloth.

Flower Frills Doily

(Continued from page 36)

and working behind next shell, make tr between 2d and 3d tr in next shell in 2d row below, inserting hook thru from back to front, ch 5, tr between next 2d and 3d tr in same way, ch 5, sc between shells in last row. Repeat from * around, join. ROW 8—* (Ch 3, tr) 6 times in ch-5 sp between next 2 tr, ch 3, sc in n xt sc between shells. Repeat from * around, join. ROW 9— Sl st to 2d sp of next shell, ch 8, tr in next sp, * (ch 3, tr) 4 times in next (center) sp, (ch 3, tr in next sp) twice, tr in 2d sp of next shell, ch 3, tr in next sp. Repeat from * around, join final tr to 5th st of ch-8. ROW 10— Repeat Row 9. ROW 11—Repeat Row 9 except make ch-2 between 2 tr in angle between shells. Join final ch-2 to 5th st of ch-8. ROW 12—* Ch 3, sk next sp, dc in next tr, (ch 3, dc in next tr) twice, (ch 3, dc) twice in next (center) sp, (ch 3, dc in next tr) 3 times, ch 3, sc in ch-2 between shells. Repeat from * around, join. ROW 13— * Ch 7 and working behind next shell, make tr between 3d and 4th tr in next shell in 2d row below, inserting hook thru from back to front, ch 5. tr between next 2d and 3d tr in same way, ch 7, sc in next sc between shells in last row. Repeat from * around, join and fasten off.

Trim—Join Green to 1st ch-3 sp on one shell, * (ch 4, sc in next sp) 4 times, ch 4, sc in same sp with last sc, (ch 4, sc in next sp) 4 times, ch 2, sc in 1st sp on next shell. Repeat from * around. Join and fasten off. ROW 2— Join Yellow to ch-2 between any 2 shells, * (ch 4, sc in next lp) 5 times, ch 4, sc in same lp with last sc, (ch 4, sc in next lp) 5 times. Repeat from * around, join and fasten off. Work 2 rows of Trim on edge of Row 6—Join Green to 1st sp on one shell, * (ch 4, sc in next sp) 3 times, ch 4, sc in same sp with last sc, (ch 4, sc in next sp) 3 times, ch 2, sc in 1st sp on next shell Repeat from * around, join. ROW 2—Join Yellow to ch-2 between any 2 shells, * (ch 4, sc in next lp) 4 times, ch 4, sc in same lp with last sc, (ch 4, sc in next lp) 3 times, ch 4, sc in ch-2 between shells. Repeat from * around, join and fasten off.

Pat back of Doily with a pad dipped in thin, hot starch. Stretch right-side-up in a true circle, pinning down between scallops in both rows of scallops. Press Center flat thru a cloth. As starch dries, pull up each shell scallop into a high point.

Irish Rose Doily

(Continued from page 38)

having 1 more ch between each tr c in each row and 1 less group of d c on each side in each row (1 group of d c left on each side), cut thread.

EDGE—Attach Green in center st of 3 d c group, * ch 4, sl st in center st of next loop, ch 3, sl st in same space, ch 4, s c in next tr c, ch 4, s c in 2nd st from hook, s d c in next st of ch, d c in next st of ch, sl st in same tr c, repeat from * 13 times, ch 4, sl st in center st of next loop, ch 3, sl st in same space, ch 4, s c in center d c of the 3 d c group, repeat from 1st * all around, join, cut thread.

Spring Garden Luncheon Set

(Continued from page 41)

other side of chain, ch 3, tr in next 3d st, (ch 3, dtr in next 3d st) 4 times, ch 3, tr in next 3d st, ch 3, dc in next 3d st, ch 3, sl st in next 3d st. ROW 2—Ch 3, 4 dc in next sp, (dc in next st, 3 dc in next sp) 8 times, dc in end st, a 4-ch p, 5 dc in next sp, (dc in next st, 4 dc in next sp) 8 times, sl st in 1st 3-ch, ch 5, 4 sc on ch, sl st in end of leaf. Fasten off.

No. 2 LEAF—Repeat No. 1 Leaf thru Row 1, then turn work over before making Row 2 (so Leaf curves in opposite direction).

PLACE MAT—Make 16 Flowers and 6 each Nos. 1 and 2

Leaves. Cut an oval paper patten 12x18 inches. Cut linen to match. Following illustration, pin flowers and leaves around edge, baste lightly and tack tog. where they meet. Working on right side, whip outside edge of motifs to linen. Turn work over, cut linen 1/4 inch from stitching, turn edge back next crochet and hem down on back of dc-row around motifs.

GLASS DOILY—Make 3 Flowers and 3 No. 2 Leaves. Cut a 5-inch circle of linen, arrange motifs as in illustration and finish as for Place Mat.

Make 4 Place Mats and 4 Glass Doilies. Stretch and pin doilies right-side-down. Steam and press dry thru a cloth.

Lily of the Valley

(Continued from page 43)

ch 5, 6 tr c cluster st in next loop, * ch 5, tr c in next loop, repeat from * 5 times, repeat from ** all around ending to correspond, join.

23rd Round. Sl st to center of loop, ch 4 and complete 6 tr c cluster st in same space, ** ch 5, 6 tr c cluster st in next loop, * ch 5, tr c in next loop, repeat from * 4 times, ch 5, d tr c in next d tr c, * ch 5, tr c in next loop, repeat from * 4 times, ch 5, 6 tr c cluster st in next loop, ch 5, 6 tr c cluster st in next loop, * ch 5, tr c in next loop, repeat from * twice, ch 5, 6 tr c cluster st in next loop, repeat from ** all around ending to correspond, join in top of 1st cluster st.

24th Round. Sl st to center of loop, ch 9, tr c in next loop, * ch 5, tr c in next loop, repeat from * 4 times, ** ch 5, d tr c in next d tr c, * ch 5, tr c in next loop, repeat from * 6 times, ch 5, work a 6 tr c cluster st in each of the next 4 loops with ch 5 between each cluster st, * ch 5, tr c in next loop, repeat from * 6 times, repeat from ** all

around ending to correspond, join in 4th st of ch.

25th Round. Sl st to center of loop, ch 9, tr c in next loop, * ch 5, tr c in next loop, repeat from * 4 times, ** ch 5, d tr c in next d tr c, * ch 5, tr c in next loop, repeat from * 18 times, repeat from ** all around ending to correspond, join.

26th Round. Ch 12, rice st in 8th st from hook (rice st: 3 tr c in same space keeping last loop of each st on hook, thread over and pull through all loops at one time), d tr c in next tr c, ch 8, rice st in top of d tr c just made, tr c in next tr c, ch 8, rice st in top of tr c just made, sl st in next tr c, ** ch 8, rice st in same space with sl st just made, tr c in next tr c, ch 8, rice st in top of tr c just made, d tr c in next tr c, ch 8, rice st in top of d tr c just made, tr c in next tr c, ch 8, rice st in top of tr c just made, sl st in next d tr c, * ch 8, rice st in same space with sl st just made, tr c in next tr c, ch 8, rice st in top of tr c just made, d tr c in next tr c, ch 8, rice st in top of d tr c just made, tr c in next tr c, ch 8, rice st in top of tr c just made, sl st in next tr c, repeat from * 3 times, repeat from ** all around ending to correspond, join, cut thread.

Simple Crochet Stitches

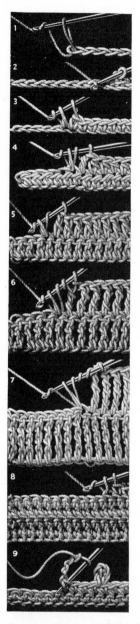

No. 1—Chain Stitch (CH) Form a loop on thread insert hook on loop and pull thread through tightening threads. Thread over hook and pull through last chain made. Continue chains for length desired.

No. 2—Slip Stitch (SL ST) Make a chain the desired length. Skip one chain, * insert hook in next chain, thread over hook and pull through stitch and loop on hook. Repeat from *. This stitch is used in joining and whenever an invisible stitch is required.

No. 3—Single Crochet (S C) Chain for desired length, skip 1 ch, * insert hook in next ch, thread over hook and pull through ch. There are now 2 loops on hook, thread over hook and pull through both loops, repeat from *. For succeeding rows of s c, ch 1, turn insert hook in top of next st taking up both threads and continue same as first row.

No. 4—Short Double Crochet (S D C) Ch for desired length thread over hook, insert hook in 3rd st from hook, draw thread through (3 loops on hook), thread over and draw through all three loops on hook. For succeeding rows, ch 2, turn.

No. 5—Double Crochet (D C) Ch for desired length, thread over hook, insert hook in 4th st from hook, draw thread through (3 loops on hook) thread over hook and pull through 2 loops thread over hook and pull through 2 loops. Succeeding rows, ch 3, turn and work next d c in 2nd d c of previous row. The ch 3 counts as 1 d c.

No. 6—Treble Crochet (TR C) Ch for desired length, thread over hook twice insert hook in 5th ch from hook draw thread through (4 loops on hook) thread over hook pull through 2 loops thread over, pull through 2 loops, thread over, pull through 2 loops. For succeeding rows ch 4, turn and work next tr c in 2nd tr c of previous row. The ch 4 counts as 1 tr c.

No. 7—Double Treble Crochet (D TR C) Ch for desired length thread over hook 3 times insert in 6th ch from hook (5 loops on hook) and work off 2 loops at a time same as tr c. For succeeding rows ch 5 turn and work next d tr c in 2nd d tr c of previous row. The ch 5 counts as 1 d tr c.

No. 8—Rib Stitch. Work this same as single crochet but insert hook in back loop of stitch only. This is sometimes called the slipper stitch.

No. 9—Picot (P) There are two methods of working the picot. (A) Work a single crochet in the foundation, ch 3 or 4 sts depending on the length of picot desired, sl st in top of s c made. (B) Work an s c, ch 3 or 4 for picot and s c in same space. Work as many single crochets between picots as desired.

No. 10—Open or Filet Mesh (O M.) When worked on a chain work the first d c in 8th ch from hook * ch 2, skip 2 sts, 1 d c in next st, repeat from *. Succeeding rows ch 5 to turn, d c in d c, ch 2, d c in next d c, repeat from *.

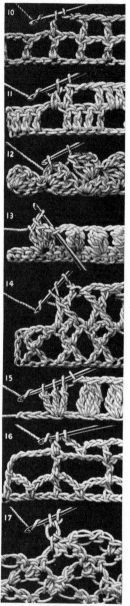

No. 11—Block or Solid Mesh (S M) Four double crochets form 1 solid mesh and 3 d c are required for each additional solid mesh. Open mesh and solid mesh are used in Filet Crochet.

No. 12—Slanting Shell St. Ch for desired length, work 2 d c in 4th st from hook, skip 3 sts, sl st in next st, * ch 3, 2 d c in same st with sl st, skip 3 sts, sl st in next st. Repeat from *. **2nd Row.** Ch 3, turn 2 d c in sl st, sl st in 3 ch loop of shell in previous row, * ch 3, 2 d c in same space, sl st in next shell, repeat from *.

No. 13—Bean or Pop Corn Stitch. Work 3 d c in same space, drop loop from hook insert hook in first d c made and draw loop through, ch 1 to tighten st.

No. 14—Cross Treble Crochet. Ch for desired length, thread over twice, insert in 5th st from hook, * work off two loops, thread over, skip 2 sts, insert in next st and work off all loops on needle 2 at a time, ch 2, d c in center to complete cross. Thread over twice, insert in next st and repeat from *.

No. 15—Cluster Stitch. Work 3 or 4 tr c in same st always retaining the last loop of each tr c on needle, thread over and pull through all loops on needle.

No. 16—Lacet St. Ch for desired length, work 1 s c in 10th st from hook, ch 3 skip 2 sts, 1 d c in next st, * ch 3, skip 2 sts, 1 s c in next st, ch 3, skip 2 sts 1 d c in next st, repeat from * to end of row, 2nd row, d c in d c, ch 5 d c in next d c.

No. 17—Knot Stitch (Sometimes Called Lovers Knot St.) Ch for desired length, * draw a ¼ inch loop on hook, thread over and pull through ch, s c in single loop of st, draw another ¼ inch loop, s c into loop, skip 4 sts, s c in next st, repeat from *. To turn make ⅜" knots, * s c in loop at right of s c and s c in loop at left of s c of previous row, 2 knot sts and repeat from *.

Metric Conversion Chart

CONVERTING INCHES TO CENTIMETERS AND YARDS TO METERS

mm — millimeters   cm — centimeters   m — meters

INCHES INTO MILLIMETERS AND CENTIMETERS
(Slightly rounded off for convenience)

inches	mm	cm	inches	cm	inches	cm	inches	cm
1/8	3mm		5	12.5	21	53.5	38	96.5
1/4	6mm		5½	14	22	56	39	99
3/8	10mm	or 1cm	6	15	23	58.5	40	101.5
1/2	13mm	or 1.3cm	7	18	24	61	41	104
5/8	15mm	or 1.5cm	8	20.5	25	63.5	42	106.5
3/4	20mm	or 2cm	9	23	26	66	43	109
7/8	22mm	or 2.2cm	10	25.5	27	68.5	44	112
1	25mm	or 2.5cm	11	28	28	71	45	114.5
1¼	32mm	or 3.2cm	12	30.5	29	73.5	46	117
1½	38mm	or 3.8cm	13	33	30	76	47	119.5
1¾	45mm	or 4.5cm	14	35.5	31	79	48	122
2	50mm	or 5cm	15	38	32	81.5	49	124.5
2½	65mm	or 6.5cm	16	40.5	33	84	50	127
3	75mm	or 7.5cm	17	43	34	86.5		
3½	90mm	or 9cm	18	46	35	89		
4	100mm	or 10cm	19	48.5	36	91.5		
4½	115mm	or 11.5cm	20	51	37	94		

YARDS TO METERS
(Slightly rounded off for convenience)

yards	meters	yards	meters	yards	meters	yards	meters	yards	meters
1/8	0.15	2⅛	1.95	4⅛	3.80	6⅛	5.60	8⅛	7.45
1/4	0.25	2¼	2.10	4¼	3.90	6¼	5.75	8¼	7.55
3/8	0.35	2⅜	2.20	4⅜	4.00	6⅜	5.85	8⅜	7.70
1/2	0.50	2½	2.30	4½	4.15	6½	5.95	8½	7.80
5/8	0.60	2⅝	2.40	4⅝	4.25	6⅝	6.10	8⅝	7.90
3/4	0.70	2¾	2.55	4¾	4.35	6¾	6.20	8¾	8.00
7/8	0.80	2⅞	2.65	4⅞	4.50	6⅞	6.30	8⅞	8.15
1	0.95	3	2.75	5	4.60	7	6.40	9	8.25
1⅛	1.05	3⅛	2.90	5⅛	4.70	7⅛	6.55	9⅛	8.35
1¼	1.15	3¼	3.00	5¼	4.80	7¼	6.65	9¼	8.50
1⅜	1.30	3⅜	3.10	5⅜	4.95	7⅜	6.75	9⅜	8.60
1½	1.40	3½	3.20	5½	5.05	7½	6.90	9½	8.70
1⅝	1.50	3⅝	3.35	5⅝	5.15	7⅝	7.00	9⅝	8.80
1¾	1.60	3¾	3.45	5¾	5.30	7¾	7.10	9¾	8.95
1⅞	1.75	3⅞	3.55	5⅞	5.40	7⅞	7.20	9⅞	9.05
2	1.85	4	3.70	6	5.50	8	7.35	10	9.15

AVAILABLE FABRIC WIDTHS

25"	65cm	50"	127cm
27"	70cm	54"/56"	140cm
35"/36"	90cm	58"/60"	150cm
39"	100cm	68"/70"	175cm
44"/45"	115cm	72"	180cm
48"	122cm		

AVAILABLE ZIPPER LENGTHS

4"	10cm	10"	25cm	22"	55cm
5"	12cm	12"	30cm	24"	60cm
6"	15cm	14"	35cm	26"	65cm
7"	18cm	16"	40cm	28"	70cm
8"	20cm	18"	45cm	30"	75cm
9"	22cm	20"	50cm		